The Twenties in America

SECOND EDITION

The Crowell American History Series

JOHN HOPE FRANKLIN & ABRAHAM S. EISENSTADT, *Editors*

The American Mind in the Mid-Nineteenth Century
IRVING H. BARTLETT

From the Old Diplomacy to the New, 1865–1900
ROBERT L. BEISNER

Parties and Politics in the Early Republic, 1789–1815
MORTON BORDEN

The Twenties in America, 2d ed.
PAUL A. CARTER

The New Deal, 2d ed.
PAUL K. CONKIN

Industrialism and the American Worker, 1865–1920
MELVYN DUBOFSKY

The Ferment of Reform, 1830–1860
C. S. GRIFFIN

The Supreme Court under Marshall and Taney
R. KENT NEWMYER

The Rise of Big Business, 1860–1910
GLENN PORTER

The American Colonies and the British Empire,
1607–1763, 2d ed.
CARL UBBELOHDE

From Isolation to War, 1931–1941
JOHN E. WILTZ

The Era of Reconstruction, 1863–1877
FORREST G. WOOD

Paul A. Carter
THE UNIVERSITY OF ARIZONA

The Twenties
in America

SECOND EDITION

Thomas Y. Crowell Company

NEW YORK

ESTABLISHED 1834

Library of Congress Cataloging in Publication Data

CARTER, PAUL ALLEN, 1926–
  The twenties in America.

  (The Crowell American history series)
  Bibliography: p.
  Includes index.
  1. United States—History—1919–1933. I. Title.
E784.C3   1975   917.3′03′915   74–26538
ISBN 0-690-00762-0

Series design by Judith Woracek Barry

Manufactured in the United States of America

For Christina, Brian, Bruce, and Robert,
born in the Sixties under LBJ,
and not at all impressed that
their father was born under
Calvin Coolidge

EDITORS' FOREWORD

It is a commonplace that each age writes its own history, for
the reason that man sees the past in the foreshortened perspective of his own experience. This has certainly been true of the
writing of American history. The purpose of our historical writing remains constant: to offer us a more certain sense of where
we are going by indicating the road we have taken in getting
there. But it is precisely because our own generation is redefin-
ing its direction, the way other generations have redefined theirs
before us, that the substance of our historical writing is changing. We are thinking anew of our direction because of our
newer values and premises, our newer sense of how we can best
fulfill the goals of our society, our newer outlook on the meaning of American life. Thus, the vitality of the present inspires
the vitality of our writing about the past.

It is the plan of the *Crowell American History Series* to offer the reader a survey of the point of arrival of recent scholarship on the central themes and problems of American history.
The scholars we have invited to do the respective volumes of the
series are younger individuals whose monographs have been
well received by their peers and who have demonstrated their
mastery of the subjects on which they are writing. The author
of each volume has undertaken to present a summation of the
principal lines of discussion that historians of a particular subject have been pursuing. However, he has not written a mere
digest of historical literature. The author has been concerned,
moreover, to offer the reader a sufficient factual and narrative
account to help him perceive the larger dimensions of the sub-

ject. Each author, moreover, has arrived at his own conclusions about those aspects of his subject that have been matters of difference and controversy. In effect, he has written not only about where the subject stands in historiography but also about where he himself stands on the subject. And each volume concludes with an extensive critical essay on authorities.

The books in this series are designed for use in the basic course in American history, although they could be used, with great benefit, in advanced courses as well. Such a series has a particular utility in times such as these, when the traditional format of our American history courses is being altered to accommodate a greater diversity of texts and reading materials. The series offers a number of distinct advantages. It extends and deepens the dimensions of course work in American history. In proceeding beyond the confines of the traditional textbook, it makes clear that the study of our past is, more than the student might otherwise infer, at once complex, sophisticated, and profound. It presents American history as a subject of continuing vitality and fresh investigation. The work of experts in their respective fields, it opens up to the student the rich findings of historical inquiry. It invites the student to join with his older and more experienced colleagues in pondering anew the major themes and problems of our past. It challenges the student to participate actively in exploring American history and to seek out its wider reaches on his own.

John Hope Franklin
Abraham S. Eisenstadt

CONTENTS

We utterly decline to be pioneers of a new age, or apostles of a new faith, or martyrs of a new war. We refuse to be psychoanalyzed. Most of us are just rather ignorant, fairly moral, quite intelligent young people, with a sense of humor and normal interests. We try to learn something from our elders but are hopelessly misled. We have open eyes, but no convictions. We don't believe politicians or preachers, but we behave as respectfully as possible and hide our smiles.

PHILIP GIBBS, The Age of Reason (1928)

ONE

Of Bohemians and Consumers

We stand at an awkward distance from the years we name the twenties. We are not quite near enough to feel their relevance to our contemporary condition, in the way we feel the relevance of Kennedy's New Frontier or Johnson's Great Society, yet we are not quite far enough away to view the decade from 1919 to 1929 with the same detachment that we contemplate the culture of the Gilded Age or the politics of Henry Clay.

No doubt this awkwardness will pass. The generation that actually experienced the twenties, with a few vigorous holdout exceptions, has by now given place to one that has only been told about them. The turning point may have been 1960, when Irving Bernstein wrote: "The present world is so far removed from the world of the twenties . . . that many who did not live through the earlier times . . . refuse to believe things were so different." A still younger generation of students may be even more ready to relegate the twenties from the realm of experience, felt as having been real, to the never-never land of history as depicted in reproductions on schoolroom walls, with George Washington (in profile) eternally crossing the Delaware.

The historian in his vocation as teacher tries to convince his hearers, caught up in the concerns of the subjective present, that what they do not themselves remember actually happened nevertheless—but historians are themselves caught up in the cycle of remembering and forgetting. So the student who would understand the twenties ought to consult both older accounts and newer: for example, Frederick Lewis Allen, writing in 1931 when the events of the previous decade had in truth taken place *Only Yesterday*, and John D. Hicks, recalling that age of *Republican Ascendancy* thirty years afterward. Such accounts support and correct each other, and newest is not necessarily truest.

In his preface to William E. Leuchtenburg's *The Perils of Prosperity 1914–32*, written in 1958, Daniel Boorstin credited the author with "the advantage of being too young to lose objectivity through his own recollections." But Leuchtenburg himself had high praise for the older work by Allen, "written," he said, "in such a lively style that academicians often underrate its soundness." True, we do need the balancing insights of the younger writer, who, in Boorstin's words, "reconstructs the . . . spirit of the age from its documents," but we need also the perspective of immediacy. Preston Slosson's *The Great Crusade and After*, for example, written in 1930 when the Prohibition amendment was a seemingly permanent part of the Constitution and the automobile was still a comparative novelty, expresses a side of the twenties which for readers since the onset of repeal and smog control would otherwise be irrecoverable. Historiography has room and need also for partisan emotion vividly recollected, as in Hicks.

In history, as in individual life, there are generation gaps. The present writer once sent a copy of an article on Senator Thomas J. Walsh of Montana, a prominent Democratic party leader in the twenties, to an aged and dear friend who had been well acquainted with the senator; with the candor of eighty years the recipient replied that she had enjoyed reading the journal, and marveled again at "the ability of trained historians to destroy almost completely the memory of persons known to the reader." Every historian should from time to time be brought up short in this fashion; as one reviewer put it, doctoral candidates in history typically prepare for scholarly work on periods prior to their own conscious lifetimes by reading a great many old newspapers—without ever quite understanding them. Distance from a man, an event, or a movement *may* grant detachment; that is why contemporary history cannot really be written as History. Distance can also deceive, either by blocking the vision of the observer with images of the intervening terrain or by blurring the further landscape in heat haze. Charles G. Sellers has written of "Andrew Jackson Versus the Historians" in words that apply with equal force to the twenties: "The succession of frames of reference and the multiplication of hypotheses can distort as well as amplify the past."

LOST GENERATION, OR JOYFUL PIONEERS?

If distance can distort, it can also enchant. In a *Harper's* article of 1954, "The Spirit of Our Times," Lovell Thompson sternly warned the older generation of his day against surrender to nostalgia about the twenties: "In spite of its wisdom, age is always deceived by its infirmity into seeing a virtue in the folly of its youth because that youth was associated with health." Still, if enchantment can distort one's vision of the past, so can disenchantment; the same infirmity which deceives age into seeing virtue in the folly of its youth can also deceive it into seeing folly in its youthful aspirations. If F. Scott Fitzgerald remained "young to the bitter end," as one postmortem essayist put it, a great many other people seem to have come out of the twenties in the same frame of mind in which they might have come out of a speakeasy, vowing "Never again!"

This sad and sober repudiation of the twenties has had at least as much publicity as the nostalgia of which Lovell Thompson complained. Thus the 1962 revision of Morison and Commager's textbook *Growth of the American Republic* left untouched its authors' earlier judgment on the twenties: "Seldom has a generation bequeathed so little that was of permanent value and so much that was troublesome to the future." The chapter to which this statement was prefatory went on to chronicle a great deal which nevertheless might be considered of permanent value: the comic genius of Charles Chaplin, the poetry of Frost and Eliot and Sandburg, the theater of O'Neill, and last but surely not least the historical scholarship of Turner and Parrington and Allan Nevins. So even the grand simplicities of a textbook, it would seem, break down before the problem of the twenties. Every generalization one makes about the period has a disconcerting way of turning into its opposite.

What confronts us here is not so much a batch of old newspapers as a kind of palimpsest, so often scrubbed and scribbled over that the *Ur*-text at the bottom is all but lost. The scribbles include slogans: "Jazz Age," "Normalcy," "Lost Generation." In his own memoir of the period, Matthew Josephson called one of the most famous among these slogans a "monumental misnomer," born of Gertrude Stein's momentary petulance at a few party crashers: "We must dispose of the fallacy of the Lost Generation once and for all," Josephson concluded. Even though he conceded Lovell Thompson's essential point—"No doubt because of the onset of age most of us think of that time as a very diverting and carefree period and so 'happier' than the present"—the historian, old or young, must also reckon with the possibility that it really *was* a diverting and carefree period for some of these people. Certainly one finds in the reminiscences of people otherwise quite different in temperament and ideology considerable evidence that alongside the "lostness" there does seem to have been a good deal of joy.

Ernest Hemingway remembered the circumstances of Miss Stein's famous remark quite differently from Josephson's account, and his posthumously published *A Moveable Feast* ended with the testimony: "This is how Paris was in the early days when we were very poor and very happy." "It wasn't that *today* was any finer in 1919 than in 1932," John Dos Passos explained, "it was that in 1919 the tomorrows seemed vaster." Joseph Wood Krutch in 1962 recalled what working for *The Nation* in the twenties had been like: "We were at bottom fundamentally optimistic, and we were gay crusaders. . . . The future was bright and the present was good fun at least." Nor is this only a reminiscence of sometime literary radicals; after all, the period dubbed itself the *New* Era, and the adjective carried the same hopeful connotations as it did when it qualified the words *Deal* and *Frontier*, however different from one another may have seemed the nouns.

"Given a chance to go forward with the policies of the last eight years," Herbert Hoover declared on being nominated for president in 1928, "we shall soon with the help of God be in sight of the day when poverty will be banished from this nation" although, as Frederick Lewis Allen pointed out, the candidate left one loophole in that acceptance speech: "It stipulated that God must assist the Republican administration." Not only Republicans and businessmen radiated optimism and confidence, impressive as is the collection of just-before-the-deluge pollyannisms uttered by bankers and stockbrokers and lovingly recorded by John Kenneth Galbraith in *The Great Crash* (3rd ed., 1972). Also the new social sciences often expressed a prophetic vision as sanguine as Hoover's. They saw a future in which all pain, misery, and maladjustment would be seen as manifestations of "culture lag," a term first popularized in the twenties; when the lag caught up with the culture, presumably, all would be well.

In a provocative essay for the *American Political Science Review*, "The Twentieth Century Enlightenment," Cushing Strout in 1955 painted a composite picture which would have fitted many a social theorist of the first third of this century, "contemptuous of the past, complacent about the present, and starry-eyed before the future," with "a touching, if narrow, faith in the efficacy of science to solve all problems and a passionate prejudice that his technical view of reason would promote progress." In the twenties "the cause of progress was not moribund but merely catching its breath," wrote Clarke Chambers in *Seedtime of Reform* (1963); in spite of setbacks and frustrations "there persisted an unending search for new ways to meet problems both old and new." The social scientists and social workers commonly wanted the exact opposite of what a businessman of the period might have considered ideal, but John Dewey was in his own way as much a booster as anybody in the chamber of commerce. Charles A. Beard sensed the unintended cultural fellow-traveling here implied, and in the preface to a characteristic tract for the times, *Whither Mankind?* he declared that the problem for the would-be reformer in the twenties was one of being optimistic without sounding like a real estate salesman.

Looking at the same problem from an entirely different angle, Hugo Gernsback in 1926 founded *Amazing Stories*, the first American magazine devoted entirely to science fiction. The second such journal came into being in 1929, and the third—the present-day *Analog*, which still tries to live down the fact that it began life as *Astounding Stories of Super Science*—was established in 1930. Magazine science fiction, as distinguished from both the consciously literary and the horror movie varieties, had in its pre-Hiroshima days a broad vein of propaganda for the Idea of Progress, with technological innovation and scientific discovery replacing Social Darwinism as history's motor mechanism; significantly, Gernsback had published some of his first science fiction in the pages of the *Electrical Experimenter*. An occasional practitioner like Howard Phillips Lovecraft might take a more Gothic tone, and the magazine *Weird Tales*, founded in 1923, in its own way shared in the literary disenchantments of the twenties; but the phrase "brave new world" had not yet acquired the overtones Aldous Huxley was to give it in 1932. A genre of popular fiction which promised many a new thing under the sun seemed a fitting accompaniment to the new age of radio.

However, the more one probes into attitudes toward progress during the twenties, the more these attitudes dissolve into ambivalence. Few spectacles were more ironic than that of Henry Ford, who was perhaps doing more to smash the old culture than any other single individual, at the same time rescuing selected relics of that culture (a Cape Cod windmill, a Mississippi paddle-wheel steamer) for the Greenfield Village museum he founded in the twenties. This ambivalence between the future and the past dogged Ford throughout his lifetime; alongside the many paeans to Ford as a progressive innovator there was also, as Allan Nevins and Frank Ernest Hill acknowledged in the second volume of their history of the Ford Motor Company, a chorus of "liberals and intellectuals who made Ford the symbol of an all-potent industrialism trampling down individuality, beauty, and serenity and erecting machine-altars to Mammon and Moloch." One of the great German silent films, *Metropolis*, included a fantastic scene in which workers in a factory of the future who lagged behind its insensate pace were fed to the machines they served; it was no coincidence that the actor cast in the leading role for this picture bore a striking physical resemblance to Ford. Even in science fiction, Prometheus the Fire Bringer transmutes easily into Frankenstein.

Was the future bright with promise, or black with foreboding? "The central paradox of American history," asserts Lawrence W. Levine, "has been a belief in progress coupled with a dread of change." Lost or otherwise, the generation of the twenties had inherited a larger stock of ideas from the Gilded Age than it ordinarily cared to admit, and that stock had included other slogans besides those of complacent optimism. Vernon Louis Parrington, in one of the brilliant unfinished passages which make the third volume of his *Main Currents in American Thought* so tantalizing, characterized the intellectual climate of the allegedly "gay" nineties as "The Darkening Skies of Letters." Larzer Ziff's more recent study of *The American 1890's* (1966) was subtitled *Life and Times of a Lost Generation*. The somber stoicism of men "left to wander . . . upon the bleak tablelands of impersonal energy," as Parrington put it, was as true a heritage from the later nineteenth century as was the humane progressivism of those whom Daniel Aaron has named the *Men of Good Hope*; the tunes in a minor key which had been learned on those "higher and bleaker tablelands of speculation" were played with great frequency during the twenties.

These would be the twenties of *The Waste Land*, of "All the Sad Young Men," and also of the sweated millhand and the disgruntled veteran—the generation which had found all the worst forebodings of its grandparents confirmed. Joseph Wood Krutch for example, even while enjoying life as a theater critic in New York, looked up from time to time at those darkening skies, and in 1929, at the existentially critical age of thirty-five, he distilled some of that darkness into an essay on *The Modern Temper*. Science, upon which some of his contemporaries pinned their hopes, could "not in any ultimate sense solve our problems," Krutch declared; on the contrary, "the more we learn of the laws of [the] universe . . . the less we shall feel at home in it." For modern man philosophy was a phantom, art no more than an opiate, tragic heroism a fallacy, and religion a lie. "We have grown used . . . to a Godless universe," he concluded one wintry chapter, "but we are not yet accustomed to one which is loveless as well, and only when we have so become shall we realize what atheism really means."

The Modern Temper, the present writer has found, still has power to break through the defenses of students against infection by a professor's ideas. However, other classroom teachers have gotten a different response: "To us," said one typical undergraduate of the radical sixties, "Mr. Krutch's pessimism seems quaint and rather sweet." Reacting to this comment, passed along to him by the student's instructor, the author of *The Modern Temper*, in his regular column for *The American Scholar*, gave himself the last word: "Since my own frame of mind is somewhat more cheerful in 1965 than it was in 1929, and since to be modern is to be much less cheerful than I was at my worst, regret at being dismissed is somewhat tempered by the realization that I could not be up-to-date without being thoroughly miserable." A still younger student generation, sharing Krutch's enthusiasm for ecology, might have found him more congenial.

Perhaps Krutch and the young disciple of "Sartre, Beckett, *et al.*" were both being unfair to the temper of the twenties. Alongside the pessimism of elegiac resignation there was also a pessimism of dialectical action: destroy the sham hopes of the world we live in to make way for a better one. Vernon Louis Parrington, who carried into the twenties the scars of older wars, wrote of "Sinclair Lewis: Our Own Diogenes" as just such a prophet of progress through deflation, rather than as the total misanthrope depicted by some of Lewis's other critics. Those merciless exposés of business fatuity and rural boorishness had the context of a posited utopia of science and rationality, which would "exalt the test-tube and deflate the cash register," dethrone the Babbitts and elevate the Arrowsmiths.

Out of "lostness" might come liberation. So thought Parrington, then the dean of historians of American letters; ever since that time the critics, in an argument best exemplified in the polemics of Frederick Hoffman and Bernard De Voto respectively, have debated whether the nay-saying intellectuals of the twenties were engaged in destruction for the sake of creative innovation or were trapped in a comprehensive and pointless negativism. That debate has itself been criticized: "An incomplete understanding of a small group of literati has shaped the understanding of American intellectual history in the 1920's," writes Roderick Nash in *The Nervous Generation* (1971). ". . . For a great many thoughtful Americans World War One did not mean intellectual derailment. . . . Prewar ideas and ideals continued into the twenties with scarcely a hitch." The intellectuals of the twenties might have been better able to resolve such questions for themselves had they possessed a better historical memory. "The threads of continuity in the history of ideas are visible across the war years, as they are across most so-called watersheds," Nash warns.

We have already noted, at least by implication, that the chilling naturalistic vision of *The Modern Temper* was a distillate of troubled Victorian reflections on apes and angels. Similarly, the idea of a revolutionary science of society so often put forth as new in the twenties owed a great deal to the spadework in the 1870s and 1880s by American inquirers like Lewis H. Morgan, John Wesley Powell, and Lester F. Ward, and still earlier by European speculators such as Comte, Saint-Simon, and of course Marx. Other liberations, constructive and otherwise, often associated with the twenties as entirely new phenomena have been traced by Henry F. May in *The End of American Innocence* (1959) to the Greenwich Village culture of the years before the First World War, and by Ray Ginger in *Altgeld's America* (1958) to the remarkable confluence of persons, forces, and ideas in the Chicago of the nineties. The cultures of Chicago and New York and fading Boston in the nineties or the teens or the twenties cannot be fully understood except in the context of Paris under the Republic of 1870, Berlin under Wilhelm I, and London in the old age of Queen Victoria.

In the American twenties, however, people evoked the past as an unreal abstraction, conservatives tending to remember it as good (as in the slogan "Back to Normalcy"), and radicals to remember it as bad (for example, as "Puritanism"—see Hoffman's discussion of their misreading of this word). In neither case was there much awareness of the past's congruity with their own time and place, nor of the sources of supply for their own arsenals of ideas.

RADICALISM RAMPANT, OR CONSERVATISM TRIUMPHANT?

In the third volume of his all but forgotten *Cosmic Philosophy*, the would-be universal scholar John Fiske had declared: "Civilization runs in a definite path, [so] that the sum total of ideas and feelings dominant in the next generation will be the offspring of the sum total of ideas and feelings dominant in this." Commenting on that judgment toward the end of a series of lectures at Princeton in 1925 on *The Dogma of Evolution*, the physicist Louis Trenchard More remarked that if the statement were true it would "leave history forever as the great unattainable science." For "what is the sum total of ideas and feelings of a generation? If I examine myself, I am bewildered by the complexity and fugitiveness of my own ideas and feelings; those of my own generation are beyond my apprehension; and those of past generations fade into vacuity." Whatever this may amount to as a judgment about history in general—and it does sound rather like a gloss on Carl Becker's "Every man his own historian"—it is not a bad statement of the cultural climate of the twenties, and it is a reminder that however much the period derived and borrowed from the times of John Fiske there were ways in which it differed sharply. This lack of a past included the lack of a revolutionary tradition to draw on, and without it the attempt to bring about a great liberation during the twenties was inevitably crippled and impoverished. Van Wyck Brooks's famous polemic of 1920, *The Ordeal of Mark Twain*, scoring points off Grandpa for his prudery, philistinism, and barbarousness instead of prudently investing his bequest of iconoclasm, is one of the more notorious examples.

The great liberation needed all the persuasive power it could muster, even including appeals to the past; it was played out on a stage before an audience much of which was frightened, anti-intellectual, and reactionary. Tennessee wrote an antievolution law onto the books and kept it there until 1967 against all the big guns of metropolitan ridicule. Sacco and Vanzetti were debated, written about, rioted over, for seven years—and nevertheless executed. A weak Soviet Union, torn by famine and civil war, became enough of a bogeyman to alarm the United States, despite our evident political stability and apparent fiscal invincibility at that time. The Ku Klux Klan stirred to new life in 1915 and grew strong enough to dictate policies and candidates as far away from its southern home base as Indiana, Oregon, Kansas, and Maine. Intolerance, Paul L. Murphy sweepingly declared in 1964, "was an integral part of the 1920s, participated in consciously or unconsciously by the great majority of Americans," and "was specially suited to the peculiar culture and society of the jazz age."

Then what becomes of the familiar stereotype of the revolt of youth during the twenties? Gilman Ostrander, writing in 1970 of *American Civilization in the First Machine Age: 1890–1940*, affirmed that the revolt was real; more specifically, that America in the 1920s was on the verge of becoming a "technological filiarchy," in which change occurs with such sweeping rapidity that only the younger generation really understands what is going on—and the old perforce, therefore, take their cues from the young. But that may be a judgment tinged by experience of the seemingly youth-oriented sixties. Perhaps in the twenties people like Van Wyck Brooks and Harold Stearns and the undergraduate subscribers to *The American Mercury* were talking primarily to one another. Abba Hillel Silver, a well-known

American rabbi, contended in 1931 that the iconoclasm of the young had been "overplayed by middle-aged moralists and lecturers" during the preceding decade; that there was in fact "no more conservative, stand-pat young man in the world than the raccoon-coated 'homo sapiens' on the American campus"; and that "in matters that really count, . . . in questions of social justice, war and peace," young Americans were "as orthodox, as unimaginative, and as submissive as the most hidebound Babbitts of their day." Their incidental bad manners might, from the standpoint of their elders, be revolting, but they did not constitute a revolt. Moreover, there were others whose judgment on reality was still more personal and private, such as the young women in college devoted primarily, in Rollene W. Saal's happy phrase, to "butterscotch sundaes, Yale boys, and Kahlil Gibran." *The Prophet* was first published in 1923, and became the most unexpected—that is, unpromoted—financial success in publishing history; it is indeed a curious book to account for as an integral part of the culture of the Jazz Age.

Arthur Schlesinger, Jr., has argued that the twenties, far from having been a decade of flaming nonconformity, were in fact a period so gray that after such a stretch of dusty conservatism people would have gone out and made a New Deal, even without the stimulus of depression, out of sheer boredom. To be sure, throughout those years voices were heard advocating liberalism, progressivism, or socialism, but in his volume of *The Economic History of the United States*, dealing with the years 1917 to 1929, George Soule asserted that "the radical movements growing out of the war had been routed, and the ferment of opinion demanding economic reconstruction had almost disappeared." This may have been an exaggeration, yet twelve years after the publication of Soule's *Prosperity Decade*, Arthur Mann entitled his account of one doughty champion of reform causes during the twenties *LaGuardia: A Fighter Against His Times*. Men and women of reforming intent who lacked the Little Flower's opportunity for responsible political life were usually more productive of inspired polemic than they were of programs for action.

Consider for example the surprising failure of the woman suffrage movement in its hour of triumph to fulfill either the hopes or the fears of Victorian and Progressive America. "The suffragists pardonably assumed that the revolution in women's status would constitute a social revolution," wrote Aileen S. Kraditor in *The Ideas of the Woman Suffrage Movement* (1965), "but in fact the enfranchisement of women did not change the economic or political structure of American society." According to William H. Chafe's study *The American Woman* (1972), the women's rights movement, lacking any new unifying and energizing issue comparable to its struggle for the vote, reached a nadir in the two decades that followed enactment of the suffrage amendment: "Beset by controversy, weakened by lack of widespread support, and torn by internecine warfare, it had ceased to exist as a powerful force."

The new freedoms of the *individual* woman in the twenties, not so much at work as at play, still fell short of the promise supposedly implicit in the Nineteenth Amendment of a cleanup of American public life in general and of politics in particular. Indeed there seems to have been some degree of regression; so formidable a woman in public life as Belle Moskowitz, a major power in Al Smith's state administration at Albany, found it politic at a Columbia University forum in April 1926 to declare her belief in the natural intellectual inferiority of women. The choice of "Maw" Ferguson as governor of Texas in a fluke runoff primary in 1924 hardly qualifies as the exception that tests the rule, for her husband had been impeached and removed from the same high office in 1917. He continued to call many of the plays in her administration, some of whose acts such as the censorship of schoolbooks for Texans bear comparison with the doings of the most Babbittish of her male political contemporaries. The reign of Mrs. Nellie Tayloe Ross as governor of

Wyoming showed more promise, but did not signify the start of a trend.

"Since the agitation for and the achievement of the franchise for women," Ida Clyde Clarke complained in a book published in 1925 with the provocative title *Uncle Sam Needs a Wife*, "he [Uncle Sam] has been courteously appointing us in negligible minorities on some of his advisory boards and commissions." Forty years later, American women would still be receiving token appointments in government or occasionally running for seats in Congress to succeed their deceased husbands. Meanwhile the proportion of women representatives in Congress and in the state legislatures steadily declined. The first woman to be elected to the United States Senate, Margaret Chase Smith, was defeated for reelection in 1972. Recently we have seen a reversal of this trend, notably with the election in 1974 of Ella Grasso as governor of Connecticut—an office she won on her own, not as a bequest from a spouse. We do not know yet whether this change of direction will last. In the twenties Americans were debating an equal rights amendment to the United States Constitution; in the midseventies the political question whether such an amendment could be ratified was still touch and go.

The historical literature of the women's rights movement itself reflects the same kind of failure: a scattering of books and monographs by women, often dismissed by male historians with epithets like "feminist," and from most of the men a deafening silence, or else paternalistic sympathy as in Page Smith's *Daughters of the Promised Land* (1971). As late as 1964 one such study, sociologist Jessie Bernard's *Academic Women*, had to be prefaced by testimonials from a leading male scholar in that woman author's own field and from her own academic dean (also, of course, male) to the effect that the book was free from axegrinding or female chauvinism. At the same time, as Page Smith notes, the percentage of women in the college academic community had declined from 38 percent in 1879 to 20 percent in 1959; furthermore, many among that 20 percent were teaching marginal courses (e.g., "bonehead" English). In the academic recession of the seventies they were to be threatened even in such time-honored bastions as home economics and women's physical education. For this long, bleak chronicle of retreat, the triumphant conversion in the twenties of segregated men's bars into integrated speakeasies scarcely sufficed as compensation.

Switzerland, that bastion of European banking, continued by ballot of its male electorate to reject woman suffrage until the end of the sixties. Although Kate Millett might have disagreed, the contrast with the example of the Soviet Union—where no particular masculine mystique seemed to be attached to practicing medicine, governing a city the size of Moscow (5 million), driving a railroad locomotive, or flying in outer space—reminds us of the old Marxist argument that full equality of the sexes would only be achieved under socialism. The twenties were scarcely a time to have attempted that solution for the United States. When Amory Blaine, in the closing pages of F. Scott Fitzgerald's *This Side of Paradise*, hitches a ride with a chauffeur-driven businessman and regales him with a vision of a socialist utopia, he is not even successful in being rude. One Fitzgerald biographer, Andrew Turnbull, has concluded that "Marxism . . . was fundamentally alien to Fitzgerald." Much that masqueraded as radicalism in the twenties was radical only in the sense of *épater les bourgeois*, using a confusedly Marxist vocabulary for much the same reason that a later generation of student radicals would use four-letter words; "even in those with a strong impulse toward dissent," Richard Hofstadter stated in *The Age of Reform* (1955), "bohemianism triumphed over radicalism."

It was not *always* pure bohemianism. Joseph North's *Robert Minor: Artist and Crusader*, produced in 1956 under the imprimatur of the American Communist party's publication arm, as

embarrassingly laudatory a biography as any company-spon-
sored sketch of the founder of a firm, nevertheless performed the
worthwhile service of reprinting two dozen of Minor's sketches
and cartoons, many of them dating from the twenties. It is to be
hoped that these savage, intensely human drawings will long
outlive the shoddy cause of American Stalinism in which Minor
was enlisted. One *Daily Worker* cartoon, for example, showed
three pudgy figures representing American, British, and French
imperialism surrounded by grinning armed giants labeled China,
India, and Africa, with the caption "Who is that you all are
going to whip, Mr. Legree?" For a later day this cartoon carried
if anything a more potent message than it had for 1925; in the
light of the tragedy of modern Southeast Asia, its message can
hardly be shrugged off as bohemian. There was, however,
enough in the radicalism of the twenties that was nihilistic,
hedonistic, or merely naughty to give Hofstadter's comment
considerable weight.

Of course, the bohemians had a point. In the pages of *The
Liberator* for December 1920, Max Eastman warned: "The
revolution will not come, or coming, it will not survive, if it
depends fundamentally upon discipline." Twenty years later, in
Stalin's Russia and the Crisis in Socialism, the former *Masses*
editor elaborated: "The essential meaning of the revolution to
me was the liberation of individuality, the extension of my
privilege of individuality to the masses of mankind." Stalin's
Russia by that time had made the idea of a disciplined socialism
for the rest of the world even less attractive for Eastman than it
had seemed in the twenties: "For my own part I have not the
glimmer of a desire to lose my identity in a collection, nor would
I wish this loss upon a single workingman." This is not
bohemianism, exactly; it calls to mind rather the Yankee
Republicanism of Robert Frost, and before this impulse was
spent it would carry Max Eastman still further to the Right.

John Dos Passos seems to have made much the same kind
of pilgrimage from Left to Right. In 1962 Daniel Aaron wrote of

Dos Passos: "It is axiomatic with him that all institutions decay; the process accelerates as managers become separated more and more from the managed." "Organization is death," Dos Passos exclaimed in 1918, contemplating enlistment in the army. Deeply involved though he was in such "radical" causes of the twenties as the Sacco-Vanzetti defense, in 1926 the novelist cautioned his friends on the Left as to what organization under the Communist party might mean: "The terrible danger to explorers is that they always find what they are looking for." Reviewing a paperback reissue of *Three Soldiers* in 1965, Robie Macauley summed up the tragic individualism that linked the "leftist" novels of John Dos Passos in the twenties and thirties with his "rightist" essays of the fifties and sixties: "All the Davids of the earlier books . . . found an opportunity to organize, won their battles, and in the process turned into new Goliaths."

To be sure, as Robert M. Crunden's *From Self to Society* (1972) and Daniel Aaron's *Writers on the Left* (1961) attest, the story did not always turn out quite that way. Much of the anarchic individualism of the twenties, chastened by the experience of the depression and by the recrudescence of international tyranny, was transformed in the early thirties into a more disciplined view of life. "There was nothing subtle about the Depression," Robert Nisbet writes; its "challenge was . . . seen to be anchored in society, in history, and not in the recesses of one's ego." Some Americans, in responding to that "powerful and determinative" challenge, became what we now nostalgically refer to as the Old Left. Mr. Krutch found *The Nation* was not so much fun to work for as his friends turned Communist, a process he watched in a frame of mind not unlike that of a civilized Roman pagan watching his friends turn Christian. For many there was eventual disillusionment. Some of Aaron's writers on the Left (for example, Granville Hicks in *Part of the Truth* [1965] and Richard Wright in his essay for *The God That Failed*, [1950]) afterward confessed to a discovery that the straitjacket of Marxism could be fully as galling as the bourgeois commercialism against which they had revolted in the first place.

The literary Stalinism of the thirties, seen in retrospect as a heartfelt reaction to the depression and fascism, retains a certain glamour. But when one reflects that in the twenties it had been far more hazardous in America to be tarred as a radical, the party lining of the following decade becomes oddly unheroic. John Reed, torn by "the choice between loyalty to an ideal and loyalty to an organization" (according to Theodore Draper's account of the last weeks of Reed's life in Russia), or the aged Eugene Debs telling the *Daily Worker* in 1924 that he was glad he had no "Vatican in Moscow" to guide him—such moments of truth give the latter-day rightist taunts of Max Eastman and John Dos Passos considerable sting. There is pathos in their recantations also. In 1964 Eastman, recalling almost wistfully a 1921 encounter with H. G. Wells, wrote: "There is—or was up to Lenin's time—a fraternity among all those who like to disturb the established inanities." The shift in verb tenses in that sentence from "is" to "was" measures with cruel accuracy the dilemma of radicalism in the twentieth century.

The dilemma had to be faced even by those among the free spirits of the twenties whose instincts were essentially Tory. Thus H. L. Mencken, ruminating on the state of the union two months before the 1920 election, confessed: "Though I am . . . in favor of property and would be quite content to see one mob of poor men (in uniform) set to gouging and hamstringing another mob of poor men (in overalls) in order to protect it, it by no means follows that I am in favor of the wealthy bounders who now run the United States." Should it come to a showdown between labor and capital in this country, Mencken predicted "a colossal victory for capitalism," which would "play off one mob against another, and pick the pockets of both"—but, the Baltimore sage ruefully added, "it will also pick *my* pockets."

After the thirties, when Mencken not only supported Alf Landon for president but so suspended his newspaperman's intuition as to persuade himself that that gentleman could be elected, a theory gained currency that Mencken had turned reactionary in his later years. (Harvey Wish, for example, continued to suggest some such change in Mencken in the final [1962] revision of his *Society and Thought in Modern America*.) Survivors from the twenties could thus remember and cherish their favorite Mencken epigrams and still regretfully drop his post-1929 writings from the canon, except for a respectful bow toward the later volumes of *The American Language*. In a still longer perspective it is becoming clear that the sage of Baltimore attacked FDR and Henry Wallace on much the same grounds that he had attacked the political leaders of the twenties, if with somewhat more bitterness and somewhat less flair. The contemporary social scene, rather than Mencken, had changed—one no longer won applause by referring to the mental processes of the working class as "a kind of insensate sweating, like that of a kidney"—and the foreign context had changed even more. Mencken's admiration of Nietzsche, Bavarian beer, and by extension all things German got by in the twenties because all Americans were presumably disillusioned with "the archangel Woodrow's" crusade to end war by downing the Hun; during the thirties and forties the term "pro-German" came, in many American minds, automatically to mean "pro-Nazi," and Mencken's laughter at the *Untermenschen* (as he viewed them) seemed to have a more sinister ring.

Still, Mencken in his great days had been admired for his opposition to many of the things the radicals of his generation also disliked: religion, Prohibition, Victorianism, commercialism, stupidity, and fraud. Indeed, the fact that he and they disliked so many of the same things may have helped to keep his memory green for a newer generation of American intellectuals recoiling from what they have called "mass culture," "*kitsch*," or "schlock" in much the same frame of mind in which Mencken had recoiled from, or rather jeered at, similar manifestations of American life in the twenties. His jibes at the New Deal forgotten if not forgiven, essays from the twenties like "Valentino," "The Sahara of the Bozart," and "The Libido for the Ugly," with its anticipation of modern discussions of urban sprawl, once again seemed as lively and relevant as they had to any reader of *The American Mercury*. To be sure, Mencken's anti-Babbittism had been uttered from a vantage point above Babbitt, as it were—that is, a vantage point not of underdog opposition but of aristocratic disdain—but perhaps this frankly aristocratic bias has helped to give these old essays their verve and bite as compared with the outpourings of more recent culture critics, unable to reconcile an essentially elitist aesthetic with their own mildly liberal (sometimes pronounced "radical") political preconceptions.

It is one of the charms and pitfalls of the twenties that elements in them which a present consensus had decided were dated and quaint have a way of suddenly coming to seem contemporary and familiar; these Mencken essays are only one example. If this is true of the high culture of that decade it is even more true of what might be called the low—the newspaper sensations, the publicizing of inconsequential personalities and events, or as Carey McWilliams once put it, "the pervading nonsense, cynicism, credulity, speakeasy wit, passion for debunkery, sex-craziness, and music-hall pornography of the times." Part of the enduring charm, and classroom utility, of Frederick Lewis Allen's *Only Yesterday* can be attributed to the fact that much of what Allen captured in 1931 before it had frozen into history still strikes many readers as fresh and alive. We turn his pages on the great court trials, on the public discussion of the revolution in morals, or on the Florida real-estate boom, and we feel that we know where we are.

SPORTS, JAZZ, AND OTHER VOCATIONS

Allen's book scores some of its strongest recognition points with readers both old and young when it dwells upon the development of athletic competitions into national mass entertainment. There is a marked contrast between the world symbolized in the pre-World War I society page treatment of Ivy League football and in Theodore Roosevelt's little moral homilies based on sports ("Don't foul, and don't shirk, and hit the line hard") on the one hand—and the elaborate apparatus of buildup, commercial tie-ins, and harmless nonsense surrounding a latter-day championship fight or bowl game, on the other. From something accessible only to an immediate local audience (except at second hand by way of telegraphed reports to the newspapers), fun and games became national in an altogether new way in the twenties thanks to the development of radio broadcasting, and have remained so ever since. The difference between the arena erected for the Jack Dempsey–Tom Gibbons fight in 1923, whose ruins remain on Montana's "high line" near Shelby to prompt philosophic reflection, and the laughably ill-executed shelter erected for the Houston Astros in 1965 is one only of degree, not of kind.

Paul Gallico's sketches of the sporting figures of the twenties (Bobby Jones, Bill Tilden, Jack Dempsey, Red Grange, Babe Ruth, and others), widely syndicated on newspaper sports pages in 1964, and similar panegyrics in the form of TV specials a decade later, made it clear that at least one aspect of the twenties still commanded a sense of psychic contemporaneity among a great many Americans. It all seemed so familiar—even the scandals, such as the 1919 "Black Sox," had echoes in boxing and college football and basketball in later years—that the reader in a world changing even more rapidly than that of the twenties clung to what by a fine irony had come to seem relatively timeless. Two- and three-platoon systems and the "lively ball" to the contrary notwithstanding, the rules and stratagems and especially the little rituals had not changed as much as had the rules and stratagems of politics, business, and war. It may have been a sign of a certain left-handed sanity in the national psyche that an American soldier, captured by the Communists in the first tense summer of the Korean War and then liberated in a counterattack by United Nations forces, brushed aside all ideological questions in his first press interview and impatiently asked, "Are the Phillies still in first place?"

This suggests that Carey McWilliams's blast at the twenties as "a period that invested the trivial with a special halo" may have been unduly harsh; better the trivial than the hysterical, perhaps. Robert K. Murray has argued that the shift of public attention in the spring of 1920 "from the antics of Lusk and Palmer to those of Dempsey and Babe Ruth" may have done more to abate the madness of the Great Red Scare of 1919 than any reasoned arguments for freedom of speech; thus it may not have been altogether a bad thing that the newspapers of the period "began to view American life not so much as a political and economic struggle but as a hilarious merry-go-round of sport, crime, and sex." Heywood Broun caught this change of mood in a fanciful essay for *The Nation*, in which he imagined the hellfire preacher John Roach Straton journeying to heaven on a hot July afternoon in 1920 to ask that fire be rained on Manhattan because forty thousand people were watching Sunday baseball in Yankee Stadium; and then, Broun reported, as Babe Ruth came up to the plate God replied to Straton, "Let's at least wait until the inning's over."

However, if the world of spectator sport during the twenties seems reassuringly familiar to the modern reader, this is not as true of other forms of mass entertainment. The present writer has observed, for example, the discomfort of a modern audience at a full-length screening, with no dubbed soundtrack and no live piano or theater organ, of the elder Douglas Fairbanks's version of *The Thief of Bagdad.* The trouble with the classics of the silent screen, for people conditioned by a more noisy, "talky" culture even than that of the twenties, is that they *are* silent. In spite of that film's ingenious and imaginative sets, striking as spectacle even by today's post-wide-screen standards, the audience, even though it was a metropolitan university foreign film crowd, literally could not take it sitting down.

Something still comes across; the crucial test is that small children, innocent of the critical moviegoer's intellectual conditioning, continue to get the message of Chaplin or the Keystone Kops or Harold Lloyd. Otherwise most of the motion pictures of the twenties seem to bring us psychically closer to the era of the gaslight and the cigar-store Indian than to our own. The great film comedies also remind our own rather humorless age that disillusionment need not be melancholy, and that denunciation may be less effective socially and politically than ridicule. Chaplin, the Kops, Lloyd, and Buster Keaton, writes Lawrence Levine in *The National Temper* (rev. ed., 1972), "did not celebrate the new age, they satirized it; . . . they did not deify the products of a consumer society, they destroyed them with willful abandon." Regrettably the solemn America of Richard Milhous Nixon and Gerald Ford sadly lacked the antic geniuses so commonplace in the twenties, who, rather than denouncing a dominant class's attitudes, in Levine's words "parodied them with hilarious accuracy."

If the movies of the twenties do not speak as readily to our present condition as do those of a later time, the legitimate stage presents a somewhat different problem. The twenties have been all but unanimously hailed as the greatest, if not the only, flowering of the theater in America, whereas the forties and fifties were conspicuously marked by notices, perhaps premature, of that medium's impending death. Indeed, if theater since the Second World War seems to have had difficulty finding itself, with the significant exception of the musical, part of the trouble may be that the theater of the twenties did its work too well. Any artistic development poses the problem to its successors: "Can you top this?" If the stage of the Jazz Age asserted freedom for normal sex (see chapters 4–8 of W. David Sievers, *Freud on Broadway*) [1955], then there was nothing left along this line for a later generation to assert except freedom for *psychopa-thia sexualis*. If Eugene O'Neill set his broodingly nihilistic philosophy in a traditional, even formalistic play structure, thereby giving it the disciplined tension that helped to make it good theater, then by the fifties it would become necessary to extend nihilism to the structure itself, so that it was not always clear that audiences were viewing plays at all. Exchanging the nihilism for politics sometimes only hastened this process, as witnesses the impassioned but sloppy guerrilla theater of the radical sixties. The theater of the absurd does have important roots in the twenties (some work of the Provincetown group; the dadaist circle in Paris; Brecht in Germany), but on the whole, when one compares *What Price Glory?* or even *Strange Interlude* with, say, *Waiting for Godot* or the works of Edward Albee, the Broadway of the twenties seems relatively homey and old-fashioned. As for the old and honored craft of acting, with the BBC leading the way it seems to have moved off the stage onto the TV tube.

What about jazz as an element of congruity between past and present? It is older than the twenties, of course, and most white Americans know by now that the only reason the period qualifies as *the* Jazz Age is that it was the time when middle-class whites first discovered this musical idiom. Gilbert Osofsky in an article for *American Quarterly* set that encounter in a wider historical context, within which the white man is perennially discovering a "new" Negro, in the case of the twenties inventing a fantasy of Harlem as Happytown to serve a function for America akin to that traditionally provided by Paris—a fantasy that repeal and depression would quickly dispel. For jazz in particular, the irony here is that militant blacks seem to have rejected identification with that form of music for the very reason that some whites accepted the medium: it was manifestly a folk, even a popular, art and was thus lowbrow.

In another *American Quarterly* article, Chadwick Hansen documents the fact that the Chicago *Defender* during the twenties invertedly accepted the white South's stereotype of jazz as "nigger music" and therefore attacked it as something blacks must live down. Dave Peyton, a columnist for that crusading Negro newspaper, wrote hopefully in 1928 that "jazz is on the wane." As for the white intelligentsia, jazz at the outset had little more prestige among them than, for example, bubblegum rock had in the early seventies, for all the valiant effort of Gilbert Seldes in *The Seven Lively Arts* (1924) to persuade them otherwise.

There were exceptions, such as the premiere of the semijazz *Rhapsody in Blue* at Aeolian Hall in New York and the recognition by Serge Koussevitsky, the elegant conductor of the Boston Symphony, that "jazz is an important contribution to modern musical literature"; there were efforts at didactic praise, such as the five paragraphs on jazz in the Beards' *Rise of American Civilization* (1927). Still there persisted for years a sense of its antithesis to all longhair music, and correspondingly a rejection of what was called jazz (loosely grouped with the society dance orchestra, radio, and popular sheet music) by professed devotees of good, that is, classical, music. Sinclair Lewis made the most benighted of his characters (in *The Man Who Knew Coolidge,* for example) enjoy jazz as a symptom of their Babbittry, and even F. Scott Fitzgerald, it seems to this reader, was slumming a bit in his references to the medium.

In the journals of news and opinion, one characteristic comment was that of Paul Poiret, a Paris fashion designer, in the *Forum* for January, 1927. Quite unlike the Frenchman of the fifties, with his taste for *le jazz hot,* M. Poiret recoiled in civilized horror from "the implacable and hypertrophic rhythms of the new dances, the blues and the Charlestons, the din of unearthly instruments, and the musical idioms of exotic lands." He predicted that "the thrall of American music, which with Paul Whiteman [!] seems to have reached its paroxysm and its zenith, will die away," and become one with "the gypsy rhythms which now seem so naïve and old-fashioned to us." The jazz of the twenties may indeed have sounded naïve and old-fashioned to rock'n'roll-attuned ears in the seventies; but who, apart from the most specialized of ethnomusicologists, was studying gypsy music with the same reverent intensity that its devotees still brought to Dixieland?

A time was coming when the tables would be turned, when the undergraduate music major would compose in a jazz idiom with the approval of his major professors, and the jazz critic, as serious in his musical purpose as Bernard Shaw and Berlioz had been in their critical essays, would become a fixture in magazines read by intellectuals. And the inevitable happened. "The advanced jazzmen," writes Wilfrid Mellers, "began to emulate the advanced straight musicians of a slightly earlier generation: they deplored the philistinism of their public, and played for themselves and their initiates." For these men too the older jazz came to be "despised as 'Jim Crow music'; and the advanced jazzmen began to . . . distinguish themselves as an elite." Meanwhile the popular culture, and the commercial media with which it is in perpetual if uneasy alliance, had recoiled against jazz as being too complex, dowdy, and intellectual. Reaching into the rhythm-and-blues subsoil whence jazz itself had come, between them these forces invented rock'n'roll. By the fifties we had come full circle; a university dean who had learned a good deal about jazz in a conscientious effort to swing with the younger generation was loftily informed by his own teenaged daughter that jazz was strictly for squares. By the seventies rock itself had already gone through more than one esoteric phase; for that very reason, some critics—perhaps hopefully?—thought it was dying.

How far away the jazz musicians and their hearers had come from the spirit of the twenties may be gauged from an incident in 1964 when, in order to keep an engagement with advanced jazzman Miles Davis without violating California law, (Davis's new percussionist being not yet twenty-one), San Francisco's Jazz Workshop surrendered its liquor license for two weeks, served soft drinks at inflated prices, and packed the house to the doors. The jazz setting of the era of Izzie and Moe—the smoky speakeasy, illegal by definition—had been an altogether different world. Although Leopold Stokowski predicted around 1925 that jazz was destined to "have the same revivifying effect as the injection of new, and in the larger sense, vulgar blood into dying aristocracy," it is rather doubtful that this fashionably dressed jazz audience, quaffing Coca-Cola or Seven-Up and politely listening, not dancing, to Mr. Davis's music, was quite what that dynamic longhair musician had had in mind. At least, unlike the uptown slummers of the twenties, this latter-day crowd was racially integrated.

Professional sports, the movies, the theater, jazz. Has our emphasis been undue, for an essay destined to be employed in work-haunted academia? In a cryptic headnote for his anthology *The Twenties: Fords, Flappers, and Fanatics* (1960)—a far better compendium than that comeon title suggests—George E. Mowry wrote: "The vast crowds that attended the sporting events of the Twenties were probably responding to something deeper than to the blandishments of the professional pitchmen." In his preface, Mowry atoned for his title by taking issue with superficial, "era-of-wonderful-nonsense" interpretations and argued that we should take the decade far more seriously than has been the custom of historians, intimating "that the Twenties were really the formative years of modern American society." Mowry's first statement might be taken as a clue to the meaning of his second. A quietly influential article by Leo Lowenthal, which first appeared in 1944 in a volume with the unpromising title *Radio Research*, has given us some insight into what the "something deeper" may have been.

Lowenthal made an intensive and imaginative study of the short, fact-studded, journalistic biographies of persons in public life to be found in the pages of the *Saturday Evening Post* and its now forgotten competitor, *Collier's Weekly*. He tabulated these biographical essays for sixteen sample years ranging between

1901 and 1941, on the hypothesis that any marked and consistent changes in subject matter and treatment might be diagnostic of change in the nature of American popular ideals, and thus perhaps of the national character. His findings, for so modest an undertaking, were rather startling. Lowenthal's article contained in germ many of the theories of social change in America which were to be put forth in the fifties: change from an inner-directed to an other-directed character in society; from an old, free professional to a new, bureaucratized middle class; from a Protestant ethic to a social ethic, or a fun morality; from a society based on an economics of scarcity to an affluent society; and from an aesthetic polarized between high and low cultures to a bland "Midcult" that threatened to swallow both. More limited in what it overtly describes than most of these later studies, the Lowenthal monograph is even more sweeping in what it implies, and the present writer therefore digests it here without further apology.

In the first place, in Lowenthal's earliest sample, for the year 1901, the subjects of these popular biographical articles were overwhelmingly people who had achieved success in workaday or enterprising ways: the immigrant scientist, the industrial or financial leader, the serious artist or writer, the prominent candidate for high office. By 1941, the proportion of essays on such persons had declined sharply; as a matter of fact, since the scientists and businessmen and statesmen in the last of the samples tended to be marginal or bizarre—for example, Ponzi, the fraudulent financier, and Brinkley, the goat-gland specialist—one might say that the percentage had shrunk to insignificance. Meanwhile, the representative men held up to the attention of a mass audience had come to consist overwhelmingly of professional athletes and people from the entertainment world—ballplayers, stars and starlets, boxers, a sideshow barker, and a gorilla named Toto. Lowenthal called his earlier batch of biographical subjects "idols of production" and his later sample "idols of consumption," inferring from these categories a major transformation of American national aspirations. However devoted to initiative, rugged individualism, and productive enterprise our public rhetoric remained in theory, in the imaginative world of these biographies "the real battlefield of history recedes from view or becomes a stock backdrop while society disintegrates into an amorphous crowd of consumers."

Moreover, Lowenthal argued, in addition to holding up idols of consumption rather than of production for attention and superlative esteem, the authors of such articles had drastically changed their conception of how their subjects got to the top. The life history of the hero at the turn of the century had been modeled on the myth of the self-made man, well within the Benjamin Franklin, Horatio Alger, log-cabin-to-presidency tradition. An individual, born and reared in obscurity or under handicap (for example, Theodore Roosevelt's asthma, George Washington Carver's race), strives toward success and, through qualities of his own character—strength, skill, intelligence, courage, or painstaking thoroughness—in due course achieves his goal. The hero of the Aspirin Age, said his magazine biographers, underwent a quite different life experience: growing up sometimes in comparable oblivion, he often suffers comparable hardships, but then gets a break. (The talent scout happens to change a travel itinerary and by chance discovers the person he is looking for, et cetera.) Success for these people is not something they achieve, but something that *happens* to them, through forces as far beyond their control as earthquake or flood: "the success of our heroes of consumption is itself goods of consumption."

Consequently, the heroes of this consumer society are no longer held up as models for imitation by the reader. "There is no road left to him for an identification with the great, or for an attempt to emulate their success." No road, that is, except the palliative of identifying with them as fellow consumers. So the biographers painstakingly note that for all their fame and fortune these public figures use the same kind of toothpaste or deodorant that John Doe does. The reader's distance from the hero's dizzying heights is bridged not by implicit admonition to go and do likewise but by the comforting reminder that in little ways we are all alike.

One could argue of course that this newer way of treating public or private lives was simply an echo in popular biography of the greater realism which had long been coming into serious literature. The real world of the nineteenth century had after all been a world whose successful few, not whose unsuccessful many, had fashioned its myths. Lowenthal did concede that the mass society of the twentieth century may be more accurately described as it has been by these magazine biographers, as a busywork world of pointless small sufferings and satisfactions punctuated occasionally for elect individuals by "the breaks," than it could ever have been portrayed in a literature of emulation, but the abandonment of an ideal, even if it be illusory, can have profound behavioral consequences; even Marx and Engels, one must remember, had argued that a shift in the ideological superstructure of society can dialectically interact with the base.

At the same time, that concrete material base of society does remain decisive, and not only for Marxists. "Man does not live by bread alone," Norman Thomas once preached, "but he does live by bread." For this very reason the Lowenthal thesis, derived from a change wholly within the superstructure of ideology which nevertheless parallels a change within the base (that is, from an economy organized around primary production to an economy geared to mass consumption), seems to the present writer extraordinarily persuasive. It satisfies one's lust for philosophical concreteness without falling into the Marxist or counter-Marxist view that the world we live in is somehow somebody's fault. It is worth noting that the editorial biases of the *Saturday Evening Post* in particular for most of the period studied by Lowenthal were those of George Horace Lorimer, an unreconstructed old guard Republican who never abandoned the Horatio Alger mystique in his editorials; thus, any change in the magazine's contents would seem attributable more to real changes in the magazine purchasers' own values than to changes in what Lorimer wanted them to believe.

"The modern individual seems subjected to decisive trends," Lowenthal wrote in summation, under the influence of which "he appears no longer as a center of outwardly bound energies and actions, . . . no longer as an integral unity on whose work and efficiency might depend not only his kin's future and happiness, but at the same time, mankind's progress in general." Instead, modern man's new heroes represent "a craving for having and taking things for granted . . . for a phantasmagoria of world-wide social security . . . for an attitude which has lost any primary interest in how to invent, shape, or apply the tools leading to such purposes of mass satisfaction." That may be pushing the hypothesis further than its data warrant, but should this little study of biographies in popular magazines in fact be diagnostic of the American condition, then the twenties, with their outpouring of new kinds of consumer goods, their declining industrial labor force which nevertheless was able to produce more of those goods, their standardization and promotion of marketing by means of national mass advertising, and their critical but confused intellectual class, would be crucial for understanding so drastic a change.

Here and there in the record are clues pointing in that direction. Robert and Helen Lynd's classic *Middletown* takes on new meaning when read in the light of the Lowenthal thesis; even the statistics are there for comparison. The ever-perceptive Richard Hofstadter noted that, while the angry young men of the twenties continued the attacks on businessmen which had been a favorite sport of their Progressive predecessors, the character of the target had subtly altered. "Where the writers of the Progressive era had attacked the businessman for his economic and political role, the intellectuals of the twenties . . .

assailed him for his personal and cultural incapacities. Where once he had been speculator, exploiter, corrupter, and tyrant, he had now become boob and philistine, prude and conformist, to be dismissed with disdain." Was this shift in rhetoric an acceptance of the hard fact of prosperity, as Hofstadter implied? Or was it a dim recognition of what Thorstein Veblen had proclaimed long before, namely that this misnamed captain of industry was as much the passive, if conspicuous, consumer as any of the people whom he, through the system, exploited?

Obviously, the twenties remained a period of unabashed admiration for the idols of production, or at least of exchange. Singling out one such "rich, powerful, self-made giant," the electric utilities leader Samuel Insull, Forrest McDonald asserted that "in the hero-worshipping postwar decade, Insull became the Babe Ruth, the Jack Dempsey, the Red Grange of the business world." Yet this particular choice of metaphors suggests that the timbre of the praise of businessmen, like that of blame as noted by Hofstadter, had already begun to change. "His doings, small and large, became a great spectator sport, and they were reported and followed accordingly." Even so strongly production-oriented a study of a figure of the twenties as McDonald's *Insull* thus can lead one back to Lowenthal's "amorphous crowd of consumers"; indeed, elsewhere in the volume McDonald calls Insull "the crucial link between Phineas T. Barnum and Madison Avenue," which would seem to vitiate the case for his hero as an idol of production.

Moreover the producers themselves in the twenties were becoming more aware of the consumer. Joseph Dorfman cites one 1927 estimate that advertising expenditures amounted to $1.5 billion, an increase of 50 percent over 1921. He quotes Julius Klein, director of the Bureau of Foreign and Domestic Commerce, in 1928: "The world as a whole is still obviously in its earliest experimental stages with installment selling, with such mass distributive apparatus as chain stores and mail-order establishments, and with problems of more accurate marketappraisal estimates of potential buying power, etc." Going into debt for consumer purchases, a practice condemned in previous more frugal eras as the last refuge of the spendthrift incompetent, came to be honored as a way to raise the standard of living and stave off depression—although in 1926 one Farmer-Laborite radical objected: "The people have mortgaged their future to live in the present. Even opium would not enable a man to invent a system of that kind."

Not only cosmetics and kilowatts, but ideas also, as the perennially observant Walter Lippmann reported in his book *Public Opinion* (1922), were increasingly being packaged into marketable "stereotypes" for mass consumption—and, one might metaphorically add, paid for on the installment plan. "We are told about the world before we see it," Lippmann wrote; and, fatalistically, "The way in which the world is imagined determines at any particular moment what men will do." More than that, say Ward Cannel and June Macklin in *The Human Nature Industry* (1973), our very selves are just such stereotypes, which each and all of us manufacture according to one or more of our society's available models of human nature. Of course the Lowenthal thesis itself could easily become another of the stereotypes Lippmann described, or in Cannel's and Macklin's terms another of the stories we tell ourselves. Like any other hypothesis it ought to be dropped at once should it cease to explain facts and begin to explain them away. Applied to the twenties, however, this hypothesis, or stereotype, is richly suggestive. The superficial froth of the period may have been sprayed forth from some deep and terrifying ocean currents indeed.

The life and liberty and property and happiness of the common man throughout the world are at the absolute mercy of a few persons whom he has never seen, involved in complicated quarrels that he has never heard of.

GILBERT MURRAY, *The League of Nations and the Democratic Idea* (1921)

You just do it. Instinctively. You don't think. Your man is there and you hit him with the ball.

Y. A. TITTLE, pro quarterback, as quoted in *The New York Times* (1964)

T W O

Of Coolidge and Hemingway

At 2:39 P.M., Dallas time, on November 22, 1963, on board the Air Force jet which earlier that day had carried John F. Kennedy toward his rendezvous with death, Lyndon Baines Johnson took the oath of office as president of the United States. The old words prescribed in the Constitution had the whine of engines for accompaniment, and the new leader gave his first order as president in the laconic language of the New Frontier: "Now, let's get airborne." The contrast with the one such transfer of power which took place during the twenties is startling: the country justice of the peace, John C. Coolidge, lighting a kerosene lamp in the living room of the family farmhouse in Plymouth, Vermont, to administer the oath of office to his son, who happened to be home on vacation.

As vice-president, Calvin Coolidge has traditionally been seen as a product of one of the touching democratic accidents that can befall even the best managed of national nominating conventions. "Completely dominated by sinister predatory economic forces" as was the Republican convention of 1920 (in the judgment of the Kansas newsman William Allen White, who had covered every Republican presidential nomination since McKinley's), it was not so utterly prostrate as to grant those interests' every wish. Having swallowed Warren Harding for president, it gagged on Irvine Lenroot, the senatorial cabal's choice for vice-president, and instead rose in rebellion to nominate Coolidge.

Since the opening to scholars of the Harding Papers in 1964 this interpretation of the 1920 GOP convention, and of the Harding administration that followed, has been vigorously challenged: first by Andrew Sinclair, who argued in The Available Man (1965) that Harding was the master of his own political fortunes rather than a puppet in the hands of Harry Daugherty and the interests, and then even more comprehensively by Robert K. Murray who, in The Harding Era (1969), upset all previous estimates by pronouncing Harding's presidency a success. Nevertheless, while giving Harding high marks for winding down the war tensions remaining from the Wilson era and for major initiatives in the areas of international disarmament, agrarian relief, and executive reorganization, Murray did not go so far as to minimize or deny the scandalous behavior in public office of some of Harding's friends. Thus it may still hold true, as William Leuchtenburg has suggested, that the subsequent elevation to the chief magistracy of the genial Ohioan's dour running mate may have turned out to be a blessing in disguise for the economic masters of his party, whose luster had begun to be dimmed by mounting scandals. "Coolidge came along at a fortuitous time, just when the democratic creed was in need of a new version of an old symbol," writes Leuchtenburg, and once the decks of the ship of state had been cleared of Jess Smith, Harry Daugherty, and the rest of that jolly pirate crew, the new president "served the needs of big business and the Old Guard even better than Harding had."

To phrase his presidency as merely having served the needs of the predatory interests is a bit unfair to Coolidge; the New Englander's political style appears to have been congenial not only to big business but also to the public at large. As for the needs of the Old Guard, Coolidge does not seem to have gotten on particularly well with old guardsman Henry Cabot Lodge, who looked on him as his social inferior. Faced with a major coal strike in the opening days of his administration, Coolidge yielded the initiative in settling it to Governor Gifford Pinchot of Pennsylvania, feeling that "dynamic federal action would usurp the state's functions." Pinchot's progressive Republican admirers saw in his successful strike settlement the germ of a chance to wrest the GOP nomination in 1924 away from the president. All that happened, however, was that the Pennsylvania governor got the blame for the resulting increase in the price of coal! "Although the problems of the day called for foresight and boldness," Robert H. Zieger concludes (*Journal of American History* [1965]), "politics called for caution and inertia; Coolidge had triumphed by doing nothing." When the dramatic Teapot Dome exposures began, writes Robert James Maddox (*Journal of American History* [1967]), "a lesser man might have weakened," and either hidden "behind the self-righteous blustering of the Old Guard" or "thrown himself upon the mercies of the party's liberal wing"; but "Coolidge did neither. His lifelong habit of refusing to budge unless it was absolutely necessary paid handsome dividends. . . . He sat astride the party as he did his self-exercise mechanical horse, riding in no direction but firmly in the saddle."

Of course, there *were* voices calling for foresight and

boldness in dealing with the problems of the day, but in a period like the 1920s, according to Francis L. Broderick, "the creative squad of liberal reformers bustle and plot amazing conferences and committee meetings at which the like-minded ignore facts, smile bravely, and build for the future" and when the polls are closed they just don't have the votes. On election day of 1924 the voters, faced with the choice of either a candidate almost as conservative as Coolidge in John W. Davis, the honest corporation counsel whom the Democrats after 103 agonized ballots had chosen to represent them that year, or a third-party nominee considered radical, gave the Yankee incumbent a full four-year term in his own right. Such, at any rate, seemed to be the sentiments of those who bothered; on August 17 the venerable Springfield *Republican* complained: "There are several million people who are more interested in the big league championship races than in the differences of opinion of Calvin Coolidge, John W. Davis, and Robert M. LaFollette."

To be sure, when the Democratic party assembled for its marathon in Madison Square Garden, John D. Hicks noted in *The Republican Ascendancy*, "ten plays on Broadway had to close during the convention for lack of business." All that this proved was that politics was a better drawing card—which, if the Lowenthal thesis has any relevance for the twenties, is only what one might expect. Contemporary advertisements for radio receivers exploited the development of politics into a mass spectator sport: "Cheer with the galleries when the delegates march in! . . . Hear the pros and cons as they fight their way to a platform for you!" To some degree this process was disguised as greater democratization ("It used to be all for the delegates' wives and the 'big' folks of politics. Now it's for everybody."), but RCA did not claim that the cheers uttered in one's home beside the Radiola were going to affect the outcome.

This early example of the hard sell should remind us also that the national economy in the twenties had largely ceased to be of a kind which would have accorded with Calvin Coolidge's thrifty Yankee ideals. While the president was lecturing his press conference on the need for business and political leaders to keep in mind "the point of view of the great bulk of citizens of the country" whom Coolidge visualized in pastoral terms as "mainly responsible for keeping their houses, farms and shops in repair and maintaining them as a going concern," a thousand other voices, from the stockbroker wooing the investor to the advertiser wooing the housewife, were drowning out the traditional cautions of "Waste not, want not" and "Save for a rainy day." Historians began noticing this phenomenon early in the game: "Huge areas of American social power were now occupied by huckstering shock troops," Charles and Mary Beard wrote in 1927, and these "embattled vendors" rose to new heights of respectability and sovereignty even as they "pushed goods, desirable and noxious alike, upon a docile herd that took its codes from big type and colored plates." There is economic as well as moral meaning in William Allen White's choice of title for his biography of Calvin Coolidge, *A Puritan in Babylon*: the Yankee small-town boy, scion of the old production-oriented economy, was in effect presiding over its liquidation.

THE TALKATIVE PRESIDENT—AND HIS CRITICS

It used to be assumed that Coolidge was essentially a passive observer of this historical process rather than an active participant in it. The president uttered a few clipped New England aphorisms, always good for spicing an otherwise dull American history lecture on the politics of the twenties; he vetoed a number of constructive measures proposed by the progressive rear guard which still survived in Congress; he labored diligently to retire the debt, balance the budget, cut down on government functions ("getting rid of our war activities" was one of the ways he put this); otherwise, apart from a few pleats and tucks here and there such as the tariff and the airmail subsidies, his administration was content to let the Roaring Twenties roar on. "We never paid any attention to what the books said about Harding and Coolidge," a former student reminisces, "because we knew the professors were in a hurry to get to Roosevelt, and the term paper was going to be on the New Deal." A just criticism, as Howard Quint acknowledged in 1964 in a lecture attended by the present writer: "We know more about the Socialists and Communists in the 1920's than we do about the Republicans."

We know a little more about one of the Republicans since Quint and Robert H. Ferrell unearthed the typescript of President Coolidge's press conferences in a wooden box which had been shipped to the public library of Coolidge's home city of Northampton, Massachusetts, at the end of his second term as president, and forgotten. "You do find in Coolidge an essential dignity," says Professor Quint, who takes exception to the old stereotype, as in Irving Stone's sketch of Coolidge for *The Aspirin Age*, in which the president's reserve and shyness were confused with lack of feeling. One of the surviving members of the Coolidge press corps confessed to these new editors, "We kinda liked the old coot." In the privacy of the press conferences silent Calvin Coolidge opened up to such an extent that Quint and Ferrell entitled their edited selections from the transcript of those conferences *The Talkative President*. This garrulous Yankee (when he chose to be) turns out to have been far more skillful as a politician and more believable as a human being than the cracker barrel caricature who has appeared in lectures and textbooks for quite some time now. The Beards, who tried to puncture the silence myth in Coolidge's own lifetime ("Coolidge was in truth a facile and versatile speaker and writer," and more to the same effect), gave us a lead here which has usually been ignored.

For one thing, Coolidge appears to have used these press conferences as an instrument for shaping public opinion, fully as consciously as Franklin Roosevelt or John Kennedy. They were not the joyous fencing matches, nor the brilliant, briefed-to-the-eyebrows performances, which the latter two presidents respectively enjoyed; they did enable Coolidge to secure skillful and sympathetic accounts of his administration—better ones, as he confessed to the reporters, than he could have composed himself. Moreover, Quint and Ferrell assert, in his answers to the newsmen's questions, "the President ranged over a wide variety of subjects with a degree of expertise that historians of a later generation not always have appreciated." To be sure, his remarks "reflected a way of looking at government and politics that is completely out of fashion today." "We need a faith that is broad enough to let the people make their own mistakes," Coolidge told the Associated Press on April 22, 1924—a faith to which neither liberals nor conservatives nowadays seem inclined. When Coolidge turned his attention to the merits of a particular measure before the Congress, according to Ferrell and Quint, "his analysis of the issues could be penetrating," and whether or not in retrospect one agrees with his judgment on an issue, the talkative president often showed the "mastery over detail that every truly successful politician must possess."

Was the man more than a mere political technician? The student must answer that question from these records for himself. Was he no more than an apologist for big-business domination? Hitherto almost all historians have, for example, taken a favorable view of the congressional farm bloc's McNary-Haugen proposals, as an attempt to redress the grievous agrarian imbalance in the American economy. They have therefore considered Coolidge's (and Herbert Hoover's) vetoes of this farm legislation as reactionary behavior. However, Gary Koerselman, in a careful and exhaustive study "Herbert Hoover and the Farm Crisis of the Twenties" (Ph.d. diss., Northern Illinois University, 1971), has concluded that the McNary-Haugen proposals were intended to benefit not the family-sized farm but the food processors and big agribusiness; if Koerselman is right, then Coolidge's veto of McNary-Haugen was not a calloused action on behalf of big business, as all the textbooks say it was, but a defense of the little man against preferential class legislation, which is what Coolidge said it was. Again, on April 10, 1928, discussing a flood-control bill then pending in Congress, President Coolidge expressed a worry that the people and property in need of protection in the flood zone had been lost sight of: "It has become a scramble to take care of the railroads and the banks and the individuals that may have invested in levee bonds, and the great lumber concerns that own many thousands of acres in that locality." A month later, in the pages of *The New Republic*, Rexford Tugwell would argue that "the stronghold of Jeffersonianism has shifted from the South to the Northeast and that its latter-day prophet is Coolidge"; but the foregoing and other lines from the presidential press conferences of the man from Vermont carry also at least a faint echo from the Age of Jackson.

It is faint indeed, compared with the color and fire of the Progressive minority that fought him from the other end of Pennsylvania Avenue—if indeed it *was* a minority. Arthur Link has reminded us that "various progressive coalitions controlled Congress for the greater part of the 1920's and were always a serious threat to the conservative administrations that controlled the executive branch." Still, if Coolidge's character and opinions were anachronistic in the twenties, to a great extent so were theirs. *The Politics of Provincialism* (1968) is the way David Burner has characterized the Democratic opposition during the twenties. Even more a case in point is the LaFollette presidential candidacy of 1924. Veterans of the Bull Moose campaign and even of Populism gathered under the Progressive banner, and William Leuchtenburg quoted a LaFollette leader as having said afterward that they ought to have campaigned to the tune of "Tenting Tonight on the Old Camp Ground." Not only Calvin Coolidge but many of his opponents were also puritans in Babylon.

One recent trend in the historical interpretation of these

rebels on Capitol Hill has indeed been to treat them as throwbacks to the Progressive Era, or earlier, rather than as harbingers of the New Deal (Fiorello LaGuardia, Robert Wagner, Senior, and perhaps George Norris excepted). Marian C. McKenna's admiring biography of the "sagebrush diplomat" William E. Borah stressed his "devotion to the older America," and presented the Idaho senator's progressivism in language more appropriate to the Old Frontier than to the New: "Reverencing the political system of simpler days, he had no desire to multiply agencies and institutions, make life more complicated, and pile new bureaucracies on old ones." These are words not so very different from those of Calvin Coolidge, telling his private press conference, "We have got so many regulatory laws already that in general I feel that we would be just as well off if we didn't have any more."

Robert LaFollette's running mate in 1924, Burton K. Wheeler, illustrates the point still more dramatically. Gadfly enough to have been called "Bolshevik Burt" by the kept press of his home state, and a strenuous prosecutor (and victim!) of the Harding cronies, by a twist of fate Wheeler one day would become the floor leader of the Senate opposition to Franklin Roosevelt's Court-packing plan. In his as-told-to autobiography published in 1962, *Yankee from the West*, the Montanan maintained that he had acted consistently. He had fought the local big interests in his home town of Butte during the First World War, he had fought other big interests on the national scene in the twenties, and he had defended the independence of the judiciary against the biggest interest of all, Big Government.

Wheeler and Borah were of course western insurgents, a fact which has implications that will be followed further in our final chapter. We must bear in mind also that the easterner Al Smith had a streak of the states'-righter in him; indeed, since the Democratic party regularly invoked Jeffersonianism, with its inescapable animus against concentration, in attacks upon the Republican regimes of the twenties, the kind of criticism Arthur

Schlesinger, Jr., makes on behalf of the Opposition in *The Crisis of the Old Order* may not always be the kind which that Opposition would have made if left to its own devices. No less a "progressive" than Franklin Delano Roosevent went on record during the twenties as preferring Jefferson over Hamilton—an embarrassment historians of a later day who admired both Hamilton and FDR never satisfactorily resolved.

If historians have difficulty in resolving questions like these, history itself does resolve them, one way or another. Forces were at work in the twenties against the continuing littleness of government, forces which carried along both the Coolidge administration and its opponents in spite of themselves. The process was already well under way in Harding's time; his supposedly weak administration created the Bureau of the Budget, which, "captured by the Executive" (*Time*, January 15, 1973), eventually would have the effect of "reducing Congress to the role of making minor alterations in a hand-me-down budget produced by each administration." The fact that *Time* was criticizing a latter-day Republican regime committed to reducing the role of government, not a New Dealish regime committed to expanding it, only underscores the point.

In *William Howard Taft: Chief Justice*, Alpheus T. Mason has shown that this same generalization holds true even for so conspicuous a stand-patter as his three-hundred-pound hero. As chief justice of the United States, ex-President Taft tirelessly pushed administrative reform of the Supreme Court through a recalcitrant Congress, and "the irony of his career," concluded Mason, "is that the revisions he sponsored and pushed through to enactment should now [1965] be helpful to causes he profoundly distrusted." But the irony is still deeper. Taft's judicial opinions themselves, Stanley I. Kutler has argued (*Journal of American History* [1969]) "ultimately—and decisively—helped weigh the balance toward national power and supremacy," Taft's personal reactionary political convictions to the contrary notwithstanding.

Consider the curious fate of one so-called temporary wartime government agency. The War Finance Corporation, instead of winding up its affairs with the coming of peace, played an unexpected and useful role as a source of loans for agricultural relief in 1921, and in fact the momentum of its establishment carried the agency down to 1929. Then, as Gerald D. Nash has shown (*Mississippi Valley Historical Review* [1959]), the WFC's managing director, Eugene Meyer, succeeded in effect in reestablishing the institution under a new name, with the same functions and many of the same personnel that the wartime lending agency had had. As the Reconstruction Finance Corporation it would be a major engine of recovery under the New Deal.

Again, Donald C. Swain in a careful study *Federal Conservation Policy, 1921–1933,* has demonstrated that "contrary to widely held opinion, the national conservation program did not deteriorate in the 1920's. It expanded and matured," even "against the wishes of the Republican chief executives." In the absence of a dramatic leader like Theodore Roosevelt, the conservation movement had to be "sparked by a vigorous bureaucratic leadership," by which Swain seems to imply that once a federal bureau has reached a certain degree of maturity, prestige, and accepted usefulness it can persist and expand and even innovate in the face of widespread apathy and opposition. Richard Kirkendall and others have shown that the same generalization holds for the Department of Agriculture during the twenties, and indeed President Hoover's own research committee on *Recent Social Trends* (1933) was destined to close out his administration with the conclusion that "the further development of American government" faced the nation as "a major and unavoidable problem of modern social life."

If government expansion continued in the face of an ideology of retrenchment, so foreign entanglement continued in the face of an ideology of isolation. Writing of "The Other Side of Isolationism: The Establishment of the First World Bank,

1929–1930," (1972) Frank Costigliola has recently described the genesis of a fiscal institution whose entanglements are of decisive and planetwide significance to this day. More sweepingly William Appleman Williams, in an essay entitled "The Legend of Isolationism in the 1920's," branded the supposedly dominant ideology a myth. "Far from isolation, the foreign relations of the United States from 1920 through 1932 were marked by express and extended involvement with—and intervention in the affairs of—other nations of the world." The cautious reader should not be put off by the fact that this judgment appeared in the Marxist pages of *Science and Society*; one takes one's scholarship where one finds it, and the radical historians' work during the past decade has taught all of us a great deal. Not every student of the history of American foreign policy will accept the implications of plan and volition in the statement just quoted, but at the very least one may say that the persons officially concerned with this country's interests abroad could and did manifest the same bureaucratic entrepreneurship that Swain's conservationists displayed at home. This could be true even though they carried on some of their activities in settings as Coolidgean as the quaint old place George F. Kennan recalls the State Department had been in the twenties when he entered it, "with its law-office atmosphere, its cool dark corridors . . . its brass cuspidors, its black leather rocking chairs, and the grandfather's clock in the Secretary of State's office."

In *Prelude to Pearl Harbor: The United States Navy and the Far East, 1921–1931*, Gerald E. Wheeler has recorded an especially striking example of how much could go on even in such cozy environs. It was a time of massive cuts in the federal budget, and the navy was expensive; it was a time of worldwide naval disarmament, a trend American leaders actively supported, and the navy was battleship minded; it was a time when Calvin Coolidge could lightly discuss with his press corps a proposal to turn the Philippines over to the Japanese as a relief measure after the great Tokyo earthquake of 1923, and the navy was both respectful and suspicious of Japan. Throughout the decade the Navy Department assumed that that empire's goal was commercial and eventual political hegemony over the Far East, and that if the United States adhered to its own stated commitments in the area the two countries were headed toward collision. Consequently, the American admirals reorganized the fleet, moving most of it for the first time into the Pacific; cadged as much as they could from Congress for modernization, slyly appealing to certain historic prejudices in that body by intimating that the money was needed for defense against the British; maneuvered and planned against the day they thought was inevitably coming—planned not in terms of coast defense but of a forward encounter with the Japanese Imperial Fleet.

Publicly, the navy faced the opposition of skeptics like Senator Thomas J. Walsh, who declared in 1928 that "a war with Japan is about as likely as a war with Mars." But some civilians shared the admirals' apprehensions. In 1929 the Hearst reporter Floyd Gibbons wrote a science fiction melodrama, *The Red Napoleon*, in which he prophesied the deaths of Al Jolson, Florenz Ziegfeld, Colonel Theodore Roosevelt, Jr., and his fellow newsmen Heywood Broun and Arthur "Bugs" Baer in a bombardment of New York City by Asian invaders in 1935, while President Al Smith sent a Christmas Day message from the refugee capital in St. Louis to hard-pressed American forces dug into the ruins of Manhattan, and the aged George M. Cohan sang "Give My Regards to Broadway" over the radio to cheer them on. Gibbons's predicted enemy was a worldwide coalition under a Soviet Genghis Khan, rather than Japan alone, but the *dénouement* of this yarn must have delighted any navy buff who read it: the defeat of the combined Communist British, French, Italian, Japanese, and German fleets in a kind of super-Jutland just outside the Gulf of Mexico. A ten-page appendix gave a complete table of organization for both fleets, with the names of all the principal ships!

It is not likely that Calvin Coolidge would have diverted his mind from the cares of state by reading such tales, as two more recent American presidents notoriously did, but he does seem to have read some of the navy's own distress signals. After the failure of the naval limitation conference in Geneva in 1927, Coolidge admitted to the reporters that the economies in naval armament which he had hoped for would now not be possible, and later that year in his annual message to Congress he gave his blessing to "a considerable building program" for the navy. The building program did not actually materialize until the thirties, and one reason may have been that many people found it easy to equate the Navy Department's sober strategic concern with the Hearst newspaperman's sensationalism. If isolationism in the twenties was a myth, as William Appleman Williams would have it, it was a myth in which many devoutly believed.

Conceding the "express and extended involvement" of which Williams wrote, in a footnote to his *America's Rise to World Power* (1954), Foster Rhea Dulles at once went on to assert that "American policy during these years remained basically isolationist." Typically, Arthur H. Vandenburg, a Grand Rapids editor whose style already had something of the senatorial flavor of his later years, declared categorically in 1926 that the prime motive for "the recent rejection of the League of Nations was the incalculable obligation of a subtle Covenant which bound us, like soldiers of fortune, into all the wars of all the world—a perpetual recruit to Mars." For every American Legion post urging readiness for any eventuality there could be found in the twenties a church group vowing that America must never again go to war—and as often as not phrasing its concern for peace in terms of isolation from Europe, the place where wars were made.

"We are opposed to any official participation in purely European affairs"; so wrote Franklin Roosevelt in July 1928, and such also was the philosophy of the Republican administration he and Al Smith were then seeking to oust. Unofficial participation, particularly in European economic and fiscal affairs, was of course extensive and important; from a study such as Joseph Brandes, *Herbert Hoover and Economic Diplomacy* (1962) emerges an impression (perhaps not entirely intended by the author) of Secretary Hoover's tenure in the Commerce Department as representing a major expansion of government functions both foreign and domestic, and ironically enough in the very name of business. Herbert Feis in *The Diplomacy of the Dollar* (1950), a monograph combining brevity with wit, pointed out the inescapable limitations inherent in such an approach: the dollar, in the relative absence of other means to a vigorous assertion of either national influence or international concord, could not do the job by itself.

Alexander De Conde has proposed a useful distinction between isolation, as an American doctrine based essentially on the geopolitical facts of life in the nineteenth century, and isolation*ism,* as the attempt to maintain that doctrine (or rather, "ad hoc strategies and policies" advocated in that doctrine's name) in the face of a twentieth-century reality to which most of those facts had ceased to apply. The twentieth-century isolationists, writes De Conde, "modified some of their ideas to fit the new circumstances but they came out with nineteenth-century conclusions." Feis's example of a State Department more concerned to prevent the sale of Pilsner Brewery bonds in the United States (as being inconsistent with our Prohibition law) than to prevent the rearmament of a nationalist Germany suggests that the feeling of isolation, in its original meaning of remoteness from Europe, had extraordinary psychological persistence.

In *Felix Frankfurter Reminisces* (1960), the jurist recalled having chaired a meeting in Boston during the twenties at which Harold Laski, fresh from a recent encounter with statesmen such as Gandhi and Nehru, lectured brilliantly on the problem of British India. Afterward, when the floor was opened for discussion, the second question asked was "What does Professor

Laski think of Calvin Coolidge?" As Frankfurter vainly appealed to the audience, "Do please ask questions pertaining to India," the questioners continued to pepper the English visitor with irrelevancies: what did he think of minimum wage laws, popular election of judges, unicameralism? America First, in the twenties, seems to have been as much an inertia as an ideology.

BIG SOCIETY
AND BELITTLED RELIGION

Thus at the psychic level at least, in foreign affairs as in matters domestic, the conventional view of American political life in the twenties seems to hold up: Babylon on wheels with nobody in the driver's seat, even though there were signs that the road ahead might be rough. Ordinarily the subsequent history of the United States government has been seen by usually liberal historians as a series of attempts to grasp hold of the steering wheel, so to speak, either indirectly through the business community (Hoover, Eisenhower) or directly by the power of government (FDR, Kennedy). However, the successive frustrations of presidents—the inability of either Hoover or Roosevelt to reduce unemployment to manageable proportions until an extraneous factor, war, came to the rescue; the inability of Truman to bring into existence a Fair Deal program against the refractory will of the Congress; or the inability of Eisenhower to end the Cold War by personal diplomacy at the summit—suggest that even the most modern or strong of executives, with the charm of a Roosevelt, the crisp decisiveness of a Truman, or the flair and form of a Kennedy, have had to play to an uncomfortably great extent the role of a Coolidge at times, occupying the seat of highest power at the price of surrendering that power's full exercise.

How could it have been otherwise? In those countries where power *was* unambiguously grasped and exercised, the outcome was terror, as under Stalin, or disaster, as in Japan, or madness, as with the Nazis. To escape a like fate, the democracies' governments had to maintain control that was something less than total: they muddled, as in England, or they improvised, as in North America. The careers of Roosevelt and W. L. Mackenzie King, so different in personal political styles, make an instructive parallel here. In the payoff of the Second World War, it was these bumbling regimes and peoples that turned out to have the qualities necessary to see it through; in that light it may be wise to remember that when a contrast with Calvin Coolidge is sought, for executive energy, far-reaching purpose, and the promotion of government action throughout society, the model most readily available in the twenties was Benito Mussolini. Coolidge's comment on his own peaceful departure from high office—"We draw our Presidents from the people. It is a wholesome thing for them to return to the people. I came from them. I wish to be one of them again"—takes on added poignancy when one considers Mussolini's violent and ignominious exit from power.

Indeed, one of the paradoxes of the twenties is that under a regime as free running as that of Calvin Coolidge so many should have complained of regimentation and conformity. The complaint itself might be dismissed as a chronic one in any age of the republic's history, especially among intellectuals; as early as 1836, Gulian Verplanck had noted a tendency of the American scholar to dwell upon his society's shortcomings "with a sort of complacent disgust." Still, the Klan atrocities and the library censorship and the labor-baiting of the period were conspicuously effective. If Big Government could scarcely be blamed for these oppressions, Big Business might have seemed a likely candidate for the villain's role; it was frequently so singled out. There was certainly enough evidence on the record of the twenties, of towns dominated, union organizers beaten, and teachers dismissed, to give this charge some substance. "While a good deal of business propaganda and a good many of the activities of strictly business associations . . . had the objective

. . . of enlarging the markets for goods, services, and securities," wrote Thomas C. Cochran and William Miller in what is still one of the best histories of American industrial society, *The Age of Enterprise* (1942), "businessmen also were seeking in every possible way to direct American thinking in lines more favorable to general business purposes. . . . And on the whole, of course, they succeeded."

The application, in our first chapter, of Leo Lowenthal's sociocultural hypothesis to the twenties suggests otherwise: whether the businessmen of the twenties were the movers and shapers of society that the businessmen of the eighties had individually been is an assumption open to serious question. At least one outsider who broke into their charmed circle, beat them at their own game, and got safely out again before the stock market carried some of them down was not notably impressed by their power and prestige, though he may later on have changed his mind. "Big businessmen are the most over-rated men in the country," Joseph P. Kennedy would one day tell his sons. "Here I am, a boy from East Boston, and I took 'em."

Furthermore, it is not clear by any means that the powers such men did possess were invariably exercised in the direction of concentration and conformity. Apologists for the gargantuan automotive industry, for one example, have argued that it has generated as many new little businesses as big ones, and may even have "served to 'de-oligopolize' other sectors of the economy that were once considered lost to monopoly." As for social and personal freedom, according to John Chamberlain in *The Enterprising Americans* (1963), the automobile "has actually worked in a profound sense to save America for the little man. . . . The sixty million cars that are now [1963] traveling the American roads mean that no one is chained to any single way of life"—though urban philosophers like Lewis Mumford, as those same millions of automobiles poured into and choked the cities, might have retorted that the real problem of reconciling freedom with order begins not on the open road but at the exit ramp.

In any case, in the limitations on liberty of which Americans in the twenties complained, factors other than private enterprise were surely involved. John Dos Passos, who in those days had no great love for America's business civilization, made the central character in his novel *Manhattan Transfer* cry out, "God I wish I could blame it all on capitalism." Against both Big Business and Big Government as a force for social conformity and sometimes for individual disintegration stood what might be termed Big Society. "Under the remorseless hammering of the machine was effected a standardization of American society that daily increased in precision and completeness," wrote Charles and Mary Beard. "Nothing escaped its iron strokes. Those who apparently directed and those who labored became one in the routine."

It is important that we not fall into the same mistake that the generation of the twenties made and assume that the American cultural or economic experience was unique and isolated. As well as an American twenties there were a British, a French, a Weimar German, even a Soviet and a Japanese twenties, and much of what took place here may have been the expression, or preview, of what is likely to happen in all industrial cultures at a certain stage of development. The impersonal processes of urbanization, machine technology, and mass communication seem inescapable, whether they are nominally presided over by a Calvin Coolidge or a Ramsay Mac-Donald, a capitalist or a socialist, or for that matter a monarch or a revolutionary committee of generals. Whether these forces make specifically for *social* conformity is of course a more open question; it is always possible that William Graham Sumner was right, and that even in the Machine Age the more archaic processes he described in *Folkways* remain decisive. It is also possible, as Lewis Mumford has always maintained, that the machine rightly used is a force for both social and individual liberation, but just exactly what one means by "rightly" has become one of the central dilemmas of our time.

Whatever the precise causative agent at work, such that the individual feels bullied, or neglected, or altogether lost in modern society, one obvious way of transcending the shortcomings of any social order is available in any historical age. From the silent intimacy of the Friends' meeting to the soaring spaces of the cathedral, the many modes of traditional religion proclaim man's ultimate worth. Even within a social organization as enormous as the Roman Catholic church there is room for the prayers and concerns of an individual lighting a votive candle—but the twenties were not a particularly auspicious time to apply that kind of remedy to the patient. A YMCA survey of the religious beliefs prevalent in the American Expeditionary Force in France, published in 1920, disclosed a vagueness in the content of what was believed coupled with acrid criticism of its institutional forms; the editors concluded that if the army draftees surveyed were a representative cross section of the people then "America is not a Christian nation in any strictly religious sense."

Such continued to be the tenor of sociological inquiry. Robert and Helen Lynd, in the chapter on religious observances in their classic study *Middletown*, found that "religious life as represented by the churches is less pervasive than a generation ago," and in 1933 Hornell Hart, summarizing the topics discussed in magazines indexed in the *Reader's Guide* for his chapter in the massive cooperative study *Recent Social Trends*, concluded that "religious sanctions have been largely displaced by scientific sanctions in discussions published in leading magazines," and furthermore that "antagonistic criticism of the church, of ministers and of traditional creeds reached a maximum in 1925–1928 in general magazines, and still exceeds the volume of favorable comment." Statistics of formal allegiance to churches seemed to bear this out; in another of the chapters in the same study, C. Luther Fry conceded that "in the last twenty years . . . religious bodies have made far more impressive gains in wealth than in membership," the Roman Catholic church included. The federal government's census of religious bodies for the decade 1926–1936 disclosed that for the first time in American history the so-called "mainstream" WASP denominations in the North—for example, Methodists, Congregationalists, Presbyterians—showed an actual net membership decline.

To be sure the decline was not irreversible. After the Second World War all of the churches, for reasons about which intellectuals in and out of church are still arguing, began to grow even faster than the population, and until about 1960 seemingly to take an upsurge in prestige and felt relevance also. This development could scarcely have been foreseen in the twenties; on the basis of the evidence available to them the forecasters of *Recent Social Trends* were justified in stating that "extrapolation of trends suggests the probable further decline of interest and belief in traditional Christianity, as herein defined." Meditating upon this cycle of decline and revival, Robert T. Handy for his presidential address to the American Society of Church History in 1959 chose the title "The American Religious Depression, 1925–1935"; for Protestantism, at least—apart from the Fundamentalist wing, which will be considered in more detail in our final chapter—the phrase seems both apt and just.

Because of the "long-standing identification of Protestantism with American culture," Handy argued, that branch of organized religion in America was "left . . . quite exposed to cultural cross-currents," and was therefore peculiarly vulnerable when those currents set in a direction unfavorable to religion in general. In *The Decline and Revival of the Social Gospel*, rev. ed. (1971) the present writer has attempted to identify some of those currents: the persuasive power of popular science (what Handy calls "scientism, behaviorism, and humanism"); the eloquent anticlerical polemics of men like Mencken and Clarence Darrow; the rising generation's aversion to Prohibition, Victorian moralism, and philistinism, with all of which the churches were associated; the widespread disillusionment over the First World War, in which the churches had played a shabby propagandizing role; and their equally shabby identification with the business ethic at its most businesslike and least ethical, of which Bruce Barton's admiring biography of Christ the Go-Getter was only the most flagrant example. When the religious depression had run its course, this combination of forces would no longer be fully operative, but the successful churches of the fifties would be open to the same basic criticism as the unsuccessful churches of the twenties: they could not redeem the individual from the inhumanity of mass society because they themselves had taken on many of the lineaments of that society.

Already in the twenties the theologically more liberal churches in particular manifested a drive for keeping up with the Joneses at all costs. In the Lynds' *Middletown*, spiritual values seem to have modulated into a kind of *civisme* ("The baffling too-bigness of European wars, death, . . . ill health, business worries, and political graft . . . all shrinks at a championship basket-ball game or a Chamber of Commerce rally, and the whole business of living in Middletown suddenly 'fits' again. . . ."), even while religious joy was being displaced in the churches themselves by a brisk and cheery good fellowship more akin to that of the Elks and Kiwanis. As one minister recalled an assistant pastorate in a church at a busy intersection in Providence, Rhode Island, toward the end of the twenties: "There were Scout troops, community boys' athletics, church school athletics, social service clubs, mothers' clubs—almost every activity imaginable, and incidentally a church."

In such a church, whose pastor might refer to it quite unselfconsciously as "our plant," the tone of worship itself was bound to change. In a city church filled on a Sunday morning with an audience rather than a congregation, Herbert Schneider has observed, "the service is more of a professional performance, less a community expression or folk art" than it had been when the parish was founded on a geographic neighborhood. At its worst, the service strained to be novel and up-to-date in the same pathetic way some adults try to keep up with the nuances of teen slang, and ultimately with as little success. The traditional "hymn-sing" was rebilled on the church bulletin board as a "Snappy Song Service"; the offertory might be enlivened by having an usher blow a whistle whenever someone dropped a dollar bill in the plate (one such ministerial entrepreneur's "temple reverberated with 105 toots on that particular Sabbath," Robert Moats Miller reports); and the sermon's text was likely to be taken from the latest edition of the newspaper and its titles from the slogans of mass media advertising. There was small comfort in such a Consumers' Church for the refugee from the consumers' world.

So far these comments have applied chiefly to Protestantism. Professor Handy, following the federal census returns, noted that "Jewish congregations enjoyed a healthy growth in the 1926–36 decade," and that by 1941 the Catholic church in America had come out of the religious depression with such strength as to prompt one converted Catholic historian, Theodore Maynard, to declare: "Except for isolated 'fundamentalists' . . . Catholicism could cut through Protestantism as through so much butter." Handy adds, "Neither Judaism nor Catholicism was embarrassed by too close identification with the surrounding culture"—a bit of an understatement, considering the Klan parades and gentlemen's agreements and restriction of immigration that marked the postwar decade. Under fire in the twenties from superpatriotic groups for alleged un-Americanism, according to Aaron Abell in *American Catholicism and Social Action* (1960), the Catholic hierarchy shelved the ambitious Bishops' Program for social action which had been formulated during the First World War, "lest it be used against Catholic interests." As for Judaism, it has seemed to Nathan Glazer in *American Judaism* (1972) that that faith in twentieth-century America "is even more vulnerable to the unsettling influence of modernity than is Christianity."

The politically conscious churchman, struggling to apply his religion directly to the criticism and reformation of Big Society, was in a particularly desperate plight. After six chapters on the vicissitudes of liberalism in the Protestant churches during the twenties, the present writer concluded in 1956 that "the Social Gospel as it stood in 1920 and the decade thereafter was living on borrowed time." Robert Moats Miller, in *American Protestantism and Social Issues, 1919–1939* (1958) has dissented in part, and urged historians to use "slightly less somber hues" to depict social Christianity in the twenties, but Donald B. Meyer, in his thoughtful, somewhat Tillichian study, *The Protestant Search for Political Realism* (1960) continued to paint in chiaroscuro: "Protestantism was entering a period of complexity and defeat" at the beginning of the twenties, an era in which the social gospel vanguard would find themselves increasingly isolated both from the culture and from their fellow churchmen.

In Judaism, judging from a perceptive study by Leonard J. Mervis of "The Social Justice Movement and the American Reform Rabbi" (*American Jewish Archives* [1955]), this isolation seems to have been felt less acutely; for, whereas "individuals of other denominations have turned to social religion," Reform Judaism had committed its total self to the religious quest for social justice. On the other hand, the Catholic liberal in the twenties, "an age of retreat when holding actions, limited counter-offensives, and prayer were the only recourse," as Francis L. Broderick has put it, was in a peculiarly awkward situation.

In *Right Reverend New Dealer*, Broderick depicted the dilemma of one such liberal, Monsignor John A. Ryan. Estranged from such Catholic prelates as William Cardinal O'Connell, who threw the formidable weight of the Boston archdiocese into the 1924 state election to defeat the ratification by Massachusetts of a proposed federal child labor amendment, a man like Father Ryan was often estranged also from secular liberals over issues in which his, and the church's, stand differed from theirs. (The exchange of letters between Ryan and Norman Thomas over the Mexican crisis of 1927, published in the *Catholic Historical Review* in 1959, is an especially poignant example.) "A friend of liberal reformers, Protestant leaders, and American Catholics," Broderick summarizes, "Ryan ran the danger that each group might embarrass him with the others." All that it seemed possible for such a person to do in the twenties to resolve such a dilemma was to wait for the historical situation to change, frustrating counsel indeed for a man of action.

THE HERO
IN AN UNHEROIC AGE

Perhaps activism was out of place for reform-minded persons, religious or otherwise. Programmatic solutions of any kind to the problems of modernity may have been premature in the twenties. Clarke Chambers cites a 1929 judgment on the shaky premises of the older Progressivism by one veteran social actionist, Donald Richberg: "What was right and what was wrong more frequently required the test of scientific analysis than of popular opinion." In short, it was necessary to know before one could act. Such seems to have been the view of James Harvey Robinson in 1921 when he declared: "I have no reforms to recommend except the liberation of intelligence."

Commenting upon that statement a quarter century afterward, Morton White found Robinson's recommendation as vague as anything proposed by President Harding. However, before the still younger reader, conditioned by the actionist sixties and the antianalytical seventies, concurs too quickly in White's criticism he should remember that men like Robinson supposed that the liberation of intelligence was a real possibility. To respond to the cruelties and absurdities of one's society by writing a book on *Mind in the Making* might have been an evasion, but it was also an act of faith, in which Robinson was joined by a small army of publicists and popularizers who conscientiously wrote to instruct, entertain, and hopefully liberate the mind of the general reader or man in the street.

It was and is easy to fault such writers and their readers, as Frederick Hoffman seems to in his book on the twenties, for having sought only "a plausible substitute for the simplicity of the Sunday sermon," in the popular-science field especially. James Steele Smith, in an essay "The Day of the Popularizers: The 1920's," replies that even the most simplistic of these interpreters of human knowledge had "a happy energy . . . in striking contrast to the sober, sometimes wry weariness of many contemporary 'general writers' on science and culture, loaded down by their sense of the loneliness of intellect and the mental emptiness of crowds." This American trend was closely related to a similar British concern for popular instruction, typified in the Victorian age by Thomas Huxley's lectures on evolution before working-class audiences and in the twenties by the popular-science writings of his grandson Julian in collaboration with H. G. Wells, as well as the popular history Wells wrote on his own. W. Warren Wagar, in *H. G. Wells and the World State*, has argued that both Wells and his American equivalents (such as Robinson), usually dismissed as pamphleteers, ought to be taken seriously as a chapter in intellectual history. Indeed, in both Britain and the United States many a young reader grown older can still acknowledge an early debt to *The Outline of History* or *Why We Behave Like Human Beings* or even, Smith and Wagar might have added, *The Stars for Sam*.

The makers of popular books were not the only persons following James Harvey Robinson's recommendation. In *The Transformation of the School*, Lawrence A. Cremin has described the institutionalization during the twenties of progressive education, which had also been conceived originally as a means to the liberation of intelligence. Shorn of most of its radical, social-reconstructionist animus by the community pressures of the time—and by the introduction of principles of "scientific management" and other concepts borrowed from business (a process documented by Raymond E. Callahan in *Education and the Cult of Efficiency*)—the progressive education movement turned from socially oriented goals to expressionist and Freudian concerns for self-fulfillment. Cremin cites one educational experimenter of the twenties who explicitly rejected social change in favor of individual regeneration, for all the world like an old-fashioned evangelical revivalist: "One could do nothing with social groups as they then existed," reasoned Margaret Naumburg in 1928, "but one could do something with individuals, who would later reform the groups they joined." The school's rejoinder to Big Society, then, was not one of preachment or social action; rather, declared the authors of *The Child-Centered School* (1928), "the task of the school is to surround the child with an environment which will draw out [his] creative power." "Once the creative power had been released in a generation of American children," commented Cremin, "the authors held little fear of the future."

On the other hand, Cremin was historically aware that "the doctrine of creative self-expression raised the same problems in education as it raised elsewhere," and he sadly conceded that "in too many classrooms license began to pass for liberty, planlessness for spontaneity, recalcitrance for individuality, obfuscation for art, and chaos for education." Stow Persons was still more harsh: in twentieth-century America, he wrote in *American Minds* (1958), "it became increasingly evident that the schools and even the colleges were places where children, instead of growing up, retained the privilege of remaining children."

Richard Hofstadter, in the three trenchant chapters on education in his *Anti-intellectualism in American Life* (1963) raised a still more disturbing possibility: that progressive education in its ultimate avatar as "life adjustment" would become neither a laboratory for social experiment nor a means to individual expression, but a vehicle for domesticating children into Big Society: "to help them learn the ways of the world of consumption and hobbies" rather than "to fit them to become a disciplined part of the world of production and competition, ambition and vocation"—all of which would have astonished John Dewey, but comes to the reader of Leo Lowenthal's essay on mass idols as the fulfillment of a prophecy.

The post-Sputnik reaction against life-adjustment education produced some equally unpleasant consequences, in the tense, highly competitive, anxiety-ridden, and joyless round of existence which could be observed at all educational levels, from the nightmare of getting into a good kindergarten to the senior professor's nagging doubt that he really was a "productive scholar" after all. Said one moppet to another boarding a school bus, in the popular caricaturist Lichty's syndicated "Grin and Bear It" cartoon one day late in 1966, "Look at it this way, Otis—school is just a mouse race to prepare us for the rat race." A spate of radical educational criticism published in the past decade concurs (*Why Children Fail, The Vanishing Adolescent, Teaching as a Subversive Activity,* and others); one hopeful sign may have been that some of it was assigned and even read in schools of education.

"We weren't that way" in school, declared William C. Devane, Yale '20, in a 1965 interview. "We had time for fun." As was noted in our first chapter, any reminiscence is suspect; still, Professor Devane, who had been Dean of Yale College for twenty-five of the intervening years, made a strong case. "What the students had in those days," as the Associated Press summarized Devane's remarks, "was an air of lightheartedness, gaiety, privacy, leisure. . . . There was time for classmate Thornton Wilder to begin his playwriting and Stephen Vincent Benét his books"—and not as projects for academic credit, he might have added. F. Scott Fitzgerald after all was a Princeton dropout, but with an entirely different set of connotations from those which the word carried for a later day.

The adverse critic of the twenties might reply that the modern student, unlike his Jazz Age counterpart, had discovered that life is real, life is earnest—except for the fact that the private, leisured, and even bohemian side of life in the twenties could itself be pursued with a kind of moral earnestness. Not always—Helen Lynd has commented tellingly on the "code of the pose" in the 1920s, by which one protected oneself from being made ridiculous by invoking the all-purpose adjective "amusing." However, in his exasperating though provocative book *Yankees and God*, Chard Powers Smith categorized the seventeenth century in America as the World of the Cosmos, the eighteenth century as the World of Man, the early nineteenth century as the World of Men, and the twenties as the World of Me—all four of which, he maintained, were variations on the single theme of Puritanism!

At times indeed the pathway of the seeker after self-fulfillment in the twenties seems to have been as bestrewn with moral dos and don'ts as the way of any seventeenth-century pilgrim. Don't be old-fashioned, don't be hypocritical, don't be a prude; and, do be brave, do obey the unconscious (D. H. Lawrence's "dark gods"), and do be honest with your own mind and emotions. It is the paradox, later to be described by Sartre, of man as "condemned to be free." If individuals are totally free to act, then they are totally responsible for what they choose (elect, in the theological sense of the word) and create, in the place of God—surely a burden more terrifying than any the erstwhile Puritans had laid down, and at the same time, the most radical possible rejection of the claims of Big Society.

Are we warranted in reading a philosophical vogue that followed the Second World War back into the situation which followed the First? Roderick Nash has made a case that we are. "At the fringe of the American intellectual community stood a few really shaken minds for whom neither the old absolutism nor the new relativism and scientism sufficed as a basis for belief." Such intellectuals "began the American exploration of a point of view later labeled *existentialism*," axiomatic for which was "confrontation with human futility and the absurdity of life." In *Hemingway and the Dead Gods*, John Killinger argued that one key figure of the twenties in particular took just such a stand. Properly noting that "there has been no known liaison between him and the existentialists," apart from whatever of that philosophic spirit Ernest Hemingway may have imbibed in the same Paris bars and cafes that Sartre and his friends were later to frequent, Killinger portrayed the novelist as having been in effect an existentialist without the vocabulary.

"When you go to war as a boy," Hemingway was to write during a later war, "you have a great illusion of immortality. Other people get killed; not you. . . . Then when you are badly wounded the first time you lose that illusion." Once the illusion is lost—in terms of Sartre, once one accepts fully the fact that authentic Being is always in the shadow of Nothingness (*nada*, in Hemingway's vocabulary)—then, and then only, can one become free, knowing in Hemingway's case that "Whatever I had to do men had always done." What one does *is*, by that definition, one's morality. Morality is not given, by the culture, by the propagandists, by the Others; "glory," "honor," "hallow" for Hemingway become obscenities when they are thus applied to the awful reality of a modern battlefield. These words are made real only moment by moment in the choices and chances of the fight, and they may legitimately be remembered only as "the numbers of roads, the names of rivers, the names of regiments and the dates." "This," Killinger comments, "is existential sentiment, emphasizing the very real kinship between the philosophy of existence and the science of phenomenology: value is only in living, not in abstractions."

Of late the Hemingway vogue has faded. Even his writing style—so dreadfully easy to parody—has lost some of its former English department ascendancy. Some of the present writer's more recent students have said that they find the rich, old-fashioned Norwegian-American prose of Ole Rolväag's *Giants in the*

Earth, also written in the twenties, more readable and convincing than Hemingway's bare-bones, who-when-where-what style. Thanks to the feminist movement we have also been made painfully aware of Papa's heavy male chauvinism. Still, in the course of such backlash judgments we must not overlook the historic fact that there *was* such a vogue; Philip Young has noted that Hemingway in the twentieth century has had a considerable impact upon even those who do not like him. Nor has this impact been simply literary. As a personal adaptation for emotional survival, learned in a situation of routinized mass slaughter and applied afterward in a situation of routinized dehumanization, Hemingway's transformation of the romantic hero into the tough-hearted stoic has commended itself to many.

Speaking for "young men born between 1918, roughly, and 1924," John W. Aldridge confessed in *After the Lost Generation* (1955) that Hemingway's "impact upon us was tremendous. . . . We could follow him, ape his manner . . . through all the doubts and fears of adolescence and come out pure and untouched." The Hemingway style seemed to some a viable answer to the moral problem posed by standardized mass consumption, mindless organization, and the discipline of the time clock. Without attempting to recover the irrevocable past, Hemingway seemed to say that "in our time" the demeaning and dehumanizing forces of Big Society can be transcended by the grace of primary experience met with courage and good form.

If Aldridge and his contemporaries really did take Hemingway's words as conveying experience so exactly "that we began unconsciously to translate our own sensations into their terms and to impose on everything we did and felt the particular emotions they aroused in us," then it is indeed possible to speak of "Hemingwayism" in ideological terms; as an ideology this tough-guy philosophy is nevertheless vulnerable. Lewis Mumford as long ago as 1951 condemned in particular the rise of a "morality of the 'dead pan' " which treated "normal emotions as deplorably sentimental and strong emotions as simply hysterical or funny"—a morality which, although Mumford did not say so, probably owed something to a simplified version of the Hemingway ideology. The Hemingway code, for example (of which Killinger's analysis made a great deal), sometimes proliferates into such minutiae that it borders on the ludicrous; not only must the kill be well and cleanly done, but on the fishing trip in *Big Two-Hearted River* the coffee in the can must be well and truly boiled, and the reader begins to feel like an intruder at a Boy Scout jamboree.

Antibourgeois though the Hemingway code was intended to be, it was anticlimactically middle-class American in one important assumption, namely that hardship and violence are something one has to go out and look for. In *The Time Between the Wars* (1962) Jonathan Daniels ironically noted that Oak Park, Illinois, the home town from which the novelist went out to hunt and fight, also sent Bruce Barton out into the rather less lethal world of Madison Avenue. He might have added that some of Hemingway's other contemporaries, such as the young black writers of the Harlem Renaissance of the twenties (Countee Cullen, Langston Hughes, Claude McKay), did not have to attend bullfights or go on safaris or enlist in wars in order to have experiences rugged enough to draw upon for their art!

Leslie A. Fiedler has reminded us that the Hemingway hero, who "returns again and again to the fishing trip and the journey to the war—those two traditional evasions of domesticity and civil life," is not a new creation of the twenties but is in fact an archetype; that fictional American men perennially have recoiled from home, marriage, and maturity by shipping out for two years before the mast or descending into maelstroms or fighting the Indians in the West or harpooning whales with Queequeg. If there is truth in this vision of the American past, then the Hemingway hero or disciple in real life faced in the last third of the twentieth century a doom ironically different from the messy but dignified death the master envisioned. "Natty Bumppo gives way to the bounty-hunter, to Buffalo Bill," Fiedler wrote, "and Buffalo Bill is followed by the dude with pack animal and guide and whisky bottle, playing Indian and fleeing his wife." To put it into Leo Lowenthal's categories, or Veblen's, Big Society increasingly transforms all primary experience into goods that it vends at second hand for consumption (the mountain is closed except to licensed climbers, the suburbs swarm out over the game preserves, the prizefight turns into vaudeville, the fishing stream is now hopelessly polluted), and the dream of self-realization through the simple life of adventure and inarticulate comradeship becomes a mocking will-o'-the-wisp.

How compelling, and at the same time how ultimately quixotic such a dream could become in the twenties has been explored in an essay by John William Ward. The solo crossing of the Atlantic in 1927 by Charles A. Lindbergh seems to have furnished something of a moral catharsis for that generation of Americans. Indeed, Ward concluded, "The grubbiness of the twenties had a good deal to do with the shining quality of Lindbergh's success." "The world understood," Walter Lippmann wrote admiringly in 1929, "that here was somebody who was altogether braver than the average sensual man" or, to put it into Hemingwayese, Lindbergh had well and truly flown. Something of the spell of the *Spirit of St. Louis* could still evoke a response as late as 1967: "He flew alone. And on a single engine," said a *Time* Essay on the fortieth anniversary of Lindbergh's flight. Unlike the astronauts who were to follow him, the flier had no constant stream of radioed instructions from a Mission Control, and no instantly available expert advice if anything went wrong; only the roaring engine and the wind.

"He was the first real hero of the machine age, and in a sense the last." In that concluding phrase the *Time* essayist followed the reasoning of Professor Ward, who marked the extraordinary choice of title for the young flier's first book (it was *We*, himself and the airplane) and asked: "Was the flight the achievement of a heroic, solitary, unaided individual? Or did the flight represent the triumph of the machine, the success of an industrially organized society?" Americans in the twenties, Ward concluded, were trying to have it both ways, celebrating a pioneer tradition of individualism and at the same time the coming discipline of machine technology, a polarity Arnold Toynbee might forebodingly have called an instance of Archaism-and-Futurism.

In 1964, Lindbergh himself added an elegiac note to this discussion. As he watched the airline stewardesses bustling with their trays thirty-five thousand feet above "the same cold-water ocean I crossed in 1927," the former Lone Eagle confessed that the taming of the air into triviality by countless scheduled crossings had "dull[ed] the sense of magic I felt then in using wings. Now it is progress that impresses me in flying, rather than adventure." Yet he was not altogether convinced. Lying under an acacia tree a few days later in Kenya in the early dawn, the flier meditated upon the simplicity of airplane construction as compared with the evolution of birds, and mused that if he had to choose he "would rather have birds than airplanes." Meeting some painted and spear-wielding Masai warriors, Lindbergh reflected that the replacement of poisoned arrows by atomic bombs was not a convincing argument for the advancement of civilization. The irony is double: a man who had once been decorated by a German government which had had in mind altogether different plans for Africa now was ready in all sincerity to doubt that his own framework of life was basically superior to that of the Masai; and this confession of mistrust in Big Society appeared in the pages of one of the most massive of Big Society's media, the *Reader's Digest*. The ambivalence continued; Lindbergh and his wife watched the Apollo 11 moon shot from a Florida wildlife refuge. Later that year the aged flier sustained a minor plane crash while on an ecological mission for the Philippine government counting water buffalo. In 1974 he chose to die not in a modern hospital but in a remote, electricityless corner of Maui, facing the sea.

"Is Civilization Progress?" the aviator had asked in his *Reader's Digest* article. No doubt a high proportion of Lindbergh's contemporaries in the twenties would have answered with a resounding "yes." For every Ernest Hemingway, fleeing the complexity of Big Society and in the process stripping the language to a deceptively simple medium for the evocation of nonverbal primary experience, there was a John Dos Passos, facing up to the complexities and inventing a rhetoric which would not merely describe but would itself actually resemble the mechanized life that was its subject. "The function of poetry in a Machine Age," Hart Crane bravely declared in 1929, "is identical to its function in any other age." Poetry would fail of its contemporary function unless it could "absorb the machine . . . as naturally and as casually as trees, cattle, galleons, castles and all other human associations of the past." In the bridges and skyscrapers which such a machine technology was bringing forth, the aged Louis Sullivan saw the promise of a vigorous, humane civilization rejoicing in the full use of its powers, material and spiritual. If Sullivan's younger contemporary Lewis Mumford disapproved of some of the specific results of that technology—"fixed and stereotyped and blank, like the mind of a Robot . . . an architecture fit only for lathes and dynamos to dwell in"—still this criticism was rooted in the modern situation, not some lost utopia of Greek temples or wattled huts.

Even those most determined to come to grips with modernity had their moments of despair. "The evil institutions that accompanied the rise of the ancient city have been resurrected and magnified in our own time," Mumford would write in 1961; ". . . the emancipation from manual labor has brought about a new kind of enslavement: abject dependence upon the machine." With rueful irony, Matthew Josephson admitted in 1962 that he and those of his associates in the twenties who "had bravely announced our 'acceptance' of the Machine Age" seemed to have made little impression on Big Society: "We had the effect of a few people firing off peashooters at the unbreakable plate glass-and-steel facade of our civilization." Hart Crane, Waldo Frank wrote in a preface to the poems of that would-be bard of the Machine Age, found himself in "a jungle of machines and disintegrating values which he had no discipline or method to manage and which soon destroyed him." Three years after the Crash, Crane stepped off the stern of a New York-bound liner, three hundred miles north of Havana.

As for the singular achievement of John Dos Passos in simulating the blinking light, random encounter, film montage quality of Megalopolis in both the form and content of his *Manhattan Transfer*, it is more a dissection than an embrace. Significantly, the most positive and sympathetic character in the novel is shown in the closing pages hitchhiking out of the city, in full flight from Big Society. Dos Passos's Jimmy Herf, still buoyant as he walked out of New York in 1925, would be mutated into Vag, the hopeless wanderer beside the endless road at the end of *U.S.A.* For a writing generation also busily rejecting the "out there" world of the farm and small town, Dos Passos's implicit moral was a counsel of desperation: if the kaleidoscope of the city refracted the individual into fragments, and the face-to-face tyranny of the small town strangled him, where was he to go?

The dilemma of a youth living through the twenties, trapped between an Old Society which cramped his style and a Big Society which seemed to have no room in it for style at all, was indeed poignant, but its resolution was not to be accomplished by literati, however gifted. "The machine's sudden entrance into the garden," Leo Marx wrote in 1964, "presents a problem that ultimately belongs not to art but to politics." If the best that art in America had to offer in the twenties was the code of Ernest Hemingway, the best that politics had to offer was the code of Calvin Coolidge.

Charles Marion Russell forsook St. Louis for Montana in 1880 when he was only sixteen. . . .

Asked to address a Montana booster meeting shortly before his death in 1926, the old man was horrified to hear himself introduced as a "pioneer." Misty-eyed, he roared: "In my book, a pioneer is a man who comes to a virgin country, traps off all the fur, kills off all the wild meat, cuts down all the trees, grazes off all the grass, plows the roots up, and strings ten million miles of bob wire. A pioneer destroys things and calls it civilization. I wish to God that this country was just like it was when I first saw it, and that none of you folks were here at all!"

ALEXANDER ELIOT, *Three Hundred Years of American Painting* (1957)

THREE

Of Town and Country

Much that happened to America in the twenties has had parallels in other times. The renascent Ku Klux Klan of the twenties not only evoked memories of Reconstruction but also prefigured the renascent Klan of a day closer to our own. The sexual revolution associated with the Jazz Age brings to mind both the campus philosophers of recent years preaching freer love, and the presidential candidate of 1884, Grover Cleveland, calmly acknowledging its practice. From an unpublished sex survey, taken in 1892 but not discovered until 1973, the historian Carl Degler concluded: "Just because people didn't talk much about sex in 1890, and started talking about it in the 1920s and 1930s, may not mean people changed very much at all in their private behavior." Many other examples could be found, but from time to time in exploring the twenties one comes upon something for which there is no exact equivalent in any other period of American history. Such a phenomenon was Prohibition.

In *The Age of Reform*, Richard Hofstadter remarked that the story of the Volstead Act, for "the historian who likes to trace the development of the great economic issues and to follow the main trend of class politics," must seem "a historical detour, a meaningless nuisance, an extraneous imposition upon the main course of history." Yet it will not do to account for an historical phenomenon simply by calling it names. Lawrence W. Levine in his study of the last years of William Jennings Bryan reminded us that the political battles of the twenties, of which the one over Prohibition was one of the most bitterly fought, were fully as momentous for the participants as the more broadly phrased political and economic controversies of the Progressive Era had been for the previous generation. "To call an era marked by conflicts of this nature one of apathy or complacence is inaccurate," Levine wrote. "To millions of Americans in the Twenties these"—the struggles over Prohibition, religion, immigration, the rights of minorities—"were the conflicts and issues which were of primary importance, and it was into these channels that they poured their idealism and fervor and energy."

If one temptation of the historian is to shrug Prohibition aside as irrelevant to the major thrust of modern history, another is its opposite: to be captivated by the sheer uniqueness of the phenomenon. Andrew Sinclair titled one study of the movement *Prohibition: The Era of Excess*. But the thirties, the forties, and even the flabby fifties were in their various ways all eras of excess, and since the publication of Sinclair's book, Ray Ginger has written of the years from 1877 to 1914 in America as an *Age of Excess*; the title as applied to the period of the Eighteenth Amendment is thus not very informative. A title is not a book; what is more serious is that Sinclair, whose British background might have given him an ironic and detached view of the matter, chose retroactively to enlist in the wars of the "Wets" and the "Drys" as a partisan and impassioned Wet.

Were there no more to the Dry crusade than our postrepeal caricature of it, these polar reactions would be more understandable. But it was not a simple matter of the yokels and the old folks and the reactionaries against the cosmopolites and the young folks and the liberals. At least in the movement's incipient stages, the prohibitionists did not feel that they were fighting the drinker—not, at any rate, the working-class drinker, who was in their view a victim of social injustice, debauched by the same system that robbed him. Rather they felt they were fighting that system itself, in the spirit of any other Populist or Progressive crusader, as monographs on Prohibition like those of James H. Timberlake, Gilman Ostrander, and Norman H. Clark have made clear.

After Prohibition had become law, there was an inevitable shift in its meaning, but the older humane ideal never quite died out. Upton Sinclair, who has never been classed among the reactionaries, wrote an antiliquor novel which was published only two years before repeal, and indeed the old socialist returned to the same theme in a work of nonfiction, *The Cup of Fury*, which appeared as late as 1957. For welfare-minded persons in the twenties, Clarke Chambers has written, "Prohibition was a divisive issue, particularly for professional settlement workers and caseworkers who were increasingly torn between their sure knowledge that alcohol so often meant unhappiness for their neighbors and clients, and their commitment to personal liberty." Of the threescore busy social workers who took time to reply to a letter soliciting the support of welfare workers throughout the nation for Al Smith in 1928, forty-five declared for Hoover, including Jane Addams, seventeen for

Smith, two for Norman Thomas; "many who declared they might otherwise support Smith protested they could not vote against a man who promised the honest and efficient administration of the Eighteenth Amendment."

As a matter of fact, in this controversy the ordinary lines between liberal and conservative in American politics seem to have become hopelessly snarled. Repeal, because of its subsequent advocacy by the Roosevelt administration, is usually considered to have been a liberal cause, yet the leaders of the Association Against the Prohibition Amendment were authentic members of the American power elite (*e.g.*, Pierre and Irénée Du Pont), and a few weeks after that organization closed its doors in 1934, its work accomplished, it reopened—with the same executive secretary—as the ultrareactionary American Liberty League. Drys were quick to point out the continuity. In 1924 a memorable debate took place between the Reverend John Haynes Holmes, a lifelong spokesman for the "social gospel," and Clarence Darrow over the issue of Prohibition. Holmes justified the Volstead Act because, he argued, liquor "creates poverty, it cultivates crime, it . . . constitutes a deliberate exploitation of the weak by the strong." Then Darrow, well known as a defender of the weak against exploitation by the strong, replied in language almost identical to that used by Barry Goldwater to justify his Senate vote against the Civil Rights Act of 1964: the Volstead Act "has made spies and detectives, snooping around doors and windows. It has made informers of thousands of us." We are reminded with a considerable sense of shock that Prohibition in the twenties actually was attacked and defended with the same vehemence, including the drumfire accompaniment of violence, with which civil rights legislation was attacked and defended in the sixties.

Sinclair's book made much of the southern racist argument for Prohibition, that this restriction was one more way of keeping the Negro in his place; a Southern racist could also argue *against* Prohibition in terms of the same prejudices. Senator Oscar Underwood of Alabama, more moderate on the race question than most of his colleagues from the South, nevertheless argued in 1928 that the Wet areas of the Northeast were "justified" in making the Eighteenth Amendment virtually inoperative by massive disobedience, in the same way that he thought the areas of the South with a large Negro population and potential electorate were "justified" in making the Fourteenth Amendment practically a dead letter. Furthermore, the Alabama senator invoked traditional southern political doctrine to condemn Prohibition because it "challenged the integrity of the compact between the States" and "compelled men to live their lives in the mold prescribed by the power of government." Conversely, in a 1926 editorial the Methodist *Christian Advocate*, militantly Dry, argued against a states'-rights solution of the liquor problem: "If New York may legally define intoxicants so as to break through the Amendment which prohibits the liquor traffic, why might not South Carolina . . . define 'involuntary servitude' in such terms as would nullify that other Prohibition Amendment which outlawed slavery?"

Argument makes strange bedfellows. Walter Lippmann, poles apart from Senator Underwood on questions of civil rights but at one with him on the question of drinking rights, argued in *Harper's* for December 1926, that the nullification of an undesired law was "a normal and traditional American method of circumventing the inflexibility of the Constitution," and President Emeritus Hadley of Yale called nullification a "safety valve which helps a self-governing community avoid the alternative between tyranny and revolution." So one visualizes Americans of that period defending violation of the law on the high philosophic grounds of John C. Calhoun or, to choose a liberal metaphor, answering the bootlegger's furtive knock on the kitchen door with a sense of righteousness as assured as if they had been harboring fugitive slaves.

THE PEERLESS LEADER
AND THE GOTHAM COCKNEY

Robert Moats Miller wisely observes: "Nothing is more difficult than for an individual indifferent to a certain issue to appreciate that to others it might be of transcendent importance." Was the right to drink, or the right to be protected from the perils of drinking, really *that* important? If it was, Prohibition cannot be dismissed as an extraneous intrusion on the course of history; and if it was not, then the sense of that importance—what the progressive educators would call its "felt need"—has somehow to be accounted for.

We may understand this felt need more clearly by comparing the Wet-Dry debate with the equally vehement drug controversy of a later day. K. Austin Kerr has made this comparison explicitly, in a monograph titled *The Politics of Moral Behavior: Prohibition and Drug Abuse* (1973). Another reason for the felt importance of the liquor issue in the twenties may have been that it was one form taken by rural-urban conflict in the same period. The dry areas of the nation roughly coincided with the old Bryan country of the nineties, a point made convincingly by the maps accompanying Andrew Sinclair's book. The urban East's representatives in Congress voted to sustain Woodrow Wilson's veto of the Volstead Act, while those of the rural South and West voted to override it. The editor of the Anti-Saloon League's *Yearbook*, mindful perhaps of the old adage that the Roman Empire did not so much fall as pass out, warned in 1931 that "great city domination is the rock upon which past civilizations have been wrecked." Judging from what was said about the country and the small town in the fiction of the same period, these sentiments were cordially reciprocated in the city.

Why did the feud between town and country, which after all is universal in human history, take the specific form of Prohibition only once, and in only two nations of western

Christendom? (The other was Finland.) Perhaps the conclusions of Leo Lowenthal's mass-media study are relevant here. If in the twenties ours was truly becoming a consumer society, such that greater stress is put, figuratively and literally, on what one takes in than on what one puts out; if the linkage between the little man and the great consists essentially in the goods they consume in common (see almost any of the advertisements in *Playboy*); if indeed consumership is becoming a surrogate for concrete accomplishment, as Veblen had maintained even before the turn of the century, mentioning ceremonial drinking (and drunkenness!) as one of his anthropological examples—then one can better understand how, in the transitional twenties, the right to drink could have been regarded as being on the same exalted level with the right to vote.

The Lowenthal thesis may also be related to the rural-urban conflict of the twenties in a more direct way. The older values of the primary producer would have persisted longer in places where they remained necessary for day-to-day survival, such as the family-sized farm. Compare the discovery by David Riesman and his associates (in *Faces in the Crowd, The Lonely Crowd*'s less widely read sequel) of their purest example of an "other-directed" personality in a Hollywood press agent and of their most clear-cut specimen of the "inner-directed" type in a Vermont handicraftsman. To be sure the battle lines between the producers of grain and the consumers of alcohol were disrupted by a high volume of informal trading with the enemy, through the good offices of the Chicago mercantile association headed by "Scarface" Al Capone and a host of lesser industrialists of the hillside still and the city bathtub, but battle lines they nevertheless were.

Town and country have been putting each other down, with opposing stereotypes of the country bumpkin and the city slicker, at least since the barefoot prophets of ancient Israel left their flocks and herds in the hills to go down and denounce the sophisticated sins of Jerusalem. In more modern times the old feud was given a lease on life by the discovery of the New World. "If European society was in any sense 'urban'," wrote Eric Lampard in the *American Historical Review* (1961), "then the city was part of the bag of tricks rejected in 1776." From Jefferson, who surely was no Anti-Saloon Leaguer, to Bryan, who certainly was, that rejection persisted and in the twenties flowered in three new rural crusades against urban wickedness: Prohibition, Fundamentalism, and the campaign to defeat Al Smith.

Note that the last mentioned of these crusades is here called "the campaign to defeat Al Smith" rather than "anti-Catholicism." It used to be assumed that these were one and the same thing, until another Catholic candidate began his drive for the presidency in the late fifties; then, as historians and political reporters scented the possibility of a Kennedy victory, they began to reassess the reasons for the Smith defeat. They remembered that Walter Lippmann in 1925 had chided those who too hastily assumed that all opposition to Smith must be based on his religion, and they discovered that one Catholic writer of the period had said that what really moved some of Smith's opponents most profoundly was that "he was 'New York minded'."

Tammany Hall and Wall Street, from the remote perspective of the delta farm or the crossroads store or the mountain hamlet, looked very much like the same thing. No amount of explanation by liberal historians or political scientists could have convinced rural and small town folk that city-machine graft is somehow socially constructive whereas stock market graft is by comparison socially regressive—popular as this view has since become in historical essays, novels (particularly Edwin O'Connor's *The Last Hurrah*), and civics textbooks. On the contrary, the East, by which people in the hinterland meant the East's urban areas rather than the decaying farms, spruce forests, ponds, and hills that remained of Thoreau's East, was seen *in toto* as a parasite consuming the fruit of the productive toil of the rest of the nation. It was, as Bryan called it, the Enemy's country.

The unfairness of that image in no way detracted from its vividness, and politicians of the day attempted to reckon with it. One such attempt was the now all but forgotten presidential candidacy of Senator Thomas J. Walsh of Montana, who, as an Irish Democrat but also a westerner, a Catholic but also a Dry, was free from the stereotype of urban corruption that clung to Governor Smith. The Montanan was best known nationally for the prosecution of the Teapot Dome investigations, and as a business broker in New York who admired Walsh put it, "Al Smith is the head of an organization which has collected much more graft than that involved in the Teapot Dome." J. Leonard Bates and others have shown that Walsh got more credit in the Teapot Dome affair than he has historically deserved, and Smith himself had demonstrated that an honest man could rise through Tammany; but still, as Mark Sullivan wrote in his syndicated newspaper column for April 1, 1928, should Walsh be elected president, "no one would suspect a private wire to Tammany Hall."

In the California presidential primary, that graveyard of more than one American candidacy, Smith trounced Walsh in 1928. As a matter of fact, the consensus of historians has come to be that the governor was an unusually strong Democratic candidate in a presidential year when the country would almost certainly have gone for Hoover in any case. Samuel Lubell summed up the magnitude of the New Yorker's national political achievement in one memorable line: "Before the Roosevelt Revolution there was an Al Smith Revolution." Still, it was something of a revolution in a vacuum, for part of the tragedy of this talented inhabitant of the Empire State was that he never quite learned to take the rest of the country seriously.

In an informal campaign biography of Smith, published in 1927, Henry F. Pringle told of a journalist who asked the New York executive in an interview for some comment on public affairs which might be of interest to readers in states west of the Mississippi, and was taken aback when Al retorted: "What states *are* west of the Mississippi?" This is of course a familiar and perennial New York attitude. "After New York it's all Bridgeport," they say in show business; and at a different point along the social spectrum from Al Smith his contemporary Ford Madox Ford confessed in 1927 that except for trips to Europe he "ventures outside the charmed circle of Gotham with the timorous sensation of one inserting his toe into the sea in order to test its temperature." *New York Is Not America*, Ford entitled these musings, and the converse was also true, he thought; fleeing the cultural confinement of Main Street, "the American who settles in New York becomes at once an ex-American."

In Governor Smith the rejection of the America that was not New York did not go *that* far, but it went far enough that David Burner, in one study of the brown derby campaign of 1928, accused the "Gotham Cockney," as he called Smith, of "an exclusionist provinciality unequalled even during the bids of William Jennings Bryan." Nor was it even a liberal provincialism; Robert Moses later testified that "Smith thought about economics in many ways like a Southern conservative"—or, he might have added, like a mildly progressive Republican such as Herbert Hoover, who *was* born west of the Mississippi. Professor Burner agrees with this estimate by Moses: "On economic issues the Governor was far less adventurous than William Jennings Bryan had been early in the twenties."

Indeed, in a sense the failure of Alfred E. Smith was the failure of William Jennings Bryan, but in reverse; each man was repulsed by the other's most devoted constituents, and each had loyal followers who loved him for the enemies he had made. In their one direct encounter at Madison Square Garden in 1924, when Smith's cause was most hopeless and Bryan's most dubious, Bryan was roundly booed by his New York audience, but the Nebraskan had also been booed by Tammany's cohorts at other Democratic national conventions when his cause had been a better one. In his very first campaign of 1896, when Bryan almost single-handedly came within a half-million votes of beating McKinley's patronage, Hanna's organization, and the GOP's millions (here the present writer follows Anna Cabot Lodge's judgment on that election, not Carl Degler's), the oratorical magic seems to have worked almost everywhere except in New York City; there, the normally Democratic New York *World* described the Commoner's Manhattan appearance in contemptuous language that makes the partisanship of twentieth-century newspapers sound tame by comparison. In perspective, the man's later attempts to defend the values of his midwestern upbringing, even its biblical fundamentalism, become more humanly understandable.

Who will now say, for example, that Tammany's preferred choice as a presidential nominee in 1912 would have been better than Bryan's? Indeed, who now remembers him? In 1916, when in spite of their breach over foreign policy Bryan again campaigned for Woodrow Wilson, concentrating on the states where his own personal following was strongest—crucial states the Democratic ticket needed in order to win—the orator from the Platte afterward interpreted Wilson's victory over Hughes to mean that "the scepter has passed from New York" in an election won "by the West and the South without the aid or consent of the East." "This mood," comments Lawrence W. Levine, "which was echoed by numerous progressive Democrats throughout the country, is important for an understanding of the difficulties the Democratic party was to face in the Twenties."

We could understand those difficulties more clearly were it not for the caricature that has passed for a portrait of Bryan among American historians and men of letters. The fashion was set soon after Bryan's death by Paxton Hibben in his biography *The Peerless Leader*, itself a monument to the twenties in its debunking style, and it continued well into the fifties in *Inherit the Wind*, a stage and screen dramatization of the Scopes trial, whose authors felt obliged to invent a subplot having no basis in history, making the Bryan character not merely ignorant and pompous but a moral monster as well. If the textbooks sometimes treated him favorably, as in Morison and Commager's summary sentence, "Bryan was the link between Andrew Jackson and Franklin D. Roosevelt," the monographs until only a few years ago presented Bryan instead as the link between Jackson and Barry Goldwater, the latter being viewed, until long after the election of 1964, with a bristling and quite unacademic hostility.

Surely there is something to be said for a political leader of whom Mr. Justice Frankfurter, an astringently rational man, in his reminiscence for the Columbia University Oral History Project in 1953 could still say "Bryan was for me with reference to public affairs what some actor or actress is to an adolescent girl." With the more recent studies of Bryan by Lawrence W. Levine, Paolo Coletta, and Paul W. Glad, the balance began to be redressed. In particular Professor Levine's *Defender of the Faith*, which focused on the Great Commoner's last and most controversial ten years, flatly contradicts the previously usual image of Bryan during the twenties. In view of the general demoralization in the ranks of the postwar progressives, Levine wrote, it would be quite understandable had Bryan abandoned the humanitarian causes of his youth—"but, in fact, no such abandonment took place."

"Have faith in mankind," Bryan cried in 1922, in the midst of the apathy, cynicism, and selfishness that surrounded the Harding regime. ". . . It is easier to-day for one to be helpful to the whole world than it was a few centuries ago to be helpful to the inhabitants of a single valley." What is surprising about these lines is that they occur in a book by Bryan, *In His Image*, the main purpose of which was to refute the theory of evolution, and this in turn suggests not only that the historical portrait of William Jennings Bryan needed to be redrawn but also that our picture of his religious milieu required a few fresh brushstrokes as well.

THE APE IN
THE TREE OF KNOWLEDGE

The theory of culture lag covered a multitude of sins in the twenties, as in fact it still does. Although the prospect for religion as a whole was not invariably treated as "the future of an illusion," that of Fundamentalism (the belief in the literal inerrancy of Scripture professed by men like Bryan) almost always was, and later generations of historians and other intellectuals have inherited and perpetuated the stereotype. Concluding his very useful study *The Fundamentalist Controversy*, published in 1954, Norman Furniss wrote: "The men and women who are concerned for the cause of intellectual freedom in midcentury America are aroused by other threats than those represented by the stragglers of the once-potent fundamentalist movement." In an essay intended for use in general survey courses in American history, completed just before his untimely death in 1964, Furniss made the point even more emphatically: "After 1925 the fundamentalist movement began to falter; and by 1930, it had lost national importance." This assumption has colored most of what has been written about Fundamentalism, at least by non-Fundamentalists, ever since.

Many college freshmen in the seventies were still coming into more than one state university's biological science courses armed against Darwinist teachings by systematic Lutheran, Baptist, Christian Reformed, sometimes Roman Catholic or even Orthodox Jewish counterinstruction. The conservative Protestant campus religious organizations—usually in our day calling themselves "evangelical" because "Fundamentalist" had acquired a bad name—glowed with cheerful and militant good health. Sydney Ahlstrom, in a paper read to the American Society of Church History in 1957, hazarded a guess that Fundamentalism and "that popular piety usually associated with Norman Vincent Peale" between them must account for "at least half of America's Christian non-Roman Catholic church-membership." Louis Gasper has traced the vicissitudes of both "moderate" and "extremist" Fundamentalism since 1930 in *The Fundamentalist Movement* (1963), and in compiling material for a reappraisal of Fundamentalism during 1964–65, the present writer turned up new specimens in abundance merely by following the public record. The cliché that Fundamentalism somehow fell apart after the Scopes trial (against evidence like the prime time television presence of Billy Graham and others) is attributable mainly to the fact that in the normal course of things academic intellectuals do not meet and converse with many Fundamentalists, just as the lingering belief in some Republican circles that Roosevelt and the New Deal were a temporary aberration from which we will all return to Normalcy one day is attributable mainly to the fact that in the normal course of things such Republicans meet and converse chiefly with other Republicans.

Charles Y. Glock and Rodney Stark in *Religion and Society in Tension* (1965), have given sociological foundation to the foregoing line of reasoning. Within a parish of one of the broad mainstream churches, they argue, the orthodox communicants are likely to remain unaware of the liberalism of their fellow members "because the people they know in the congregation, their friends, do share" their conservative beliefs; conversely the liberals, tending to find their social contacts and outlets elsewhere than in the church, and thus "not being linked into the congregation by friendship bonds, may remain largely unaware of the fundamentalist segment of the congregation." The writer would only add from personal observation that the sudden awakening from this state of blissful mutual ignorance can be a shock to both parties.

The Fundamentalists *did*, in the main, lose control of the institutional and public relations machinery of the established Protestant denominations during the twenties, at least in the Northeast, but where Fundamentalism since Bryan's time has gone can be seen in any American city today. William G.

McLoughlin has warned against accepting liberal Protestant-ism's (self-interested?) evaluation of these other, non-"main-stream" churches as "minor," "backward," or "ecstatic"; on the contrary, the new pietistic Fundamentalism as it had taken shape since the midthirties was in fact "a second wing of Protestantism in America." As in the seventies, so in the twenties, in order to grasp fully the significance of Fundamental-ism it is necessary to see it as a powerful creed having vitality for millions of adherents rather than as a cranky, marginal belief doomed to a speedy extinction.

Still, do not Fundamentalism's rural antecedents support the culture lag hypothesis, since the United States from the twenties through the seventies was becoming increasingly urban-ized? "Fundamentalism," writes William E. Leuchtenburg, "made sense to men in isolated rural areas still directly dependent on nature for their livelihood; they distrusted human capacity and relied on divine intervention, because it had been their own experience that men had to rely on the rains for the crops and were all but helpless when disease struck." As agronomy and medicine and mechanization advanced, it would have been logical to expect such a religion to retreat, except for the fact that Fundamentalism's appeal was not limited to rural America.

In a paper read at the 1965 session of the American Historical Association, Ernest R. Sandeen concluded: "Funda-mentalism originated in the northeastern part of this continent in metropolitan areas and cannot be explained as a part of the populist movement, agrarian protest or the Southern mentality." McLoughlin reminds us that "in 1925, contrary to general belief, [Fundamentalism's] leadership and dynamic force came from its urban adherents." It was from a New York City pulpit that the Reverend John Roach Straton thundered at the evolutionists and at Al Smith and Sunday baseball during the twenties, and there were effective Fundamentalist ministries in those years in Boston and Philadelphia and Chicago as well as in California,

Kansas, and Tennessee. This is not to deny a natural kinship between old-time religion and the rural mind; for all that it was exaggerated by the metropolitan press the Scopes trial had *some* symbolical reality. It is rather to remind ourselves that one can be ruralist by adoption as well as by inheritance. One does not have to be born on a ranch to enjoy a western, which millions of easterners patently do, and similarly one did not have to be an old-timer to accept the old-time religion.

Into old-timer politics also one can be naturalized as well as born: witness the allegiance to Senator Goldwater down through 1964 on the part of well fed and underexercised suburban youths even less credible as rugged frontiersmen than their hero, who at least looked good on a horse. Since there was a notable upsurge of Fundamentalist political discourse specifically in connection with the 1964 presidential campaign, this almost irresistibly suggests another favorite historical stereotype of Fundamentalism: that it is nothing more than the religious version of right-wing secular politics. Ralph Roy in his biting account *Apostles of Discord*, a study of rightist hate groups of the early fifties, documented the persistence and pervasiveness of this connection, such that many warriors in the antievolution crusade of the twenties remained active in anticommunist and other crusades of more recent years; Gail Sindell described in a 1973 doctoral dissertation the ideological career of one of the most notorious such right-wing warriors, Gerald B. Winrod, whose evangelical career spanned the gap between Billy Sunday and Billy Graham; William Leuchtenburg's account of the twenties included a chapter on Ku Kluxism, anti-immigrantism, Prohibition, and the Scopes trial, all lumped together as "Political Fundamentalism."

The pivotal figure in the Scopes trial was William Jennings Bryan, and Bryan, as Willard H. Smith and Lawrence Levine have shown, retained more of a social gospel—that is, in secular terms, liberal—orientation than he has usually been given credit for. In 1919, for example, Bryan urged the Christian church not to ignore the problem of corporate monopoly; it must be the church's task "to protect the God-made man from the man-made giant." Throughout the half-decade of the twenties into which the Commoner survived, he continued to excoriate the churches for their seeming indifference to such issues as profiteering, tax exploitation, industrial injustice, and international anarchy. There are obvious objections which can be raised to this kind of religion, but they are of a radically different kind from those usually lodged against William Jennings Bryan and against Fundamentalism. We may also note that the same rural hinterland which nourished Barry Goldwater and William Jennings Bryan also produced George McGovern, whose clear-cut political moralism surely owed something to a Fundamentalist preacher-father who was active in the ministry during the twenties.

Much Fundamentalist thought during the twenties was in fact neither liberal nor conservative, but apolitical if not antipolitical. The pessimism toward society at large became so profound that the believer sought redemption *from* it, not *of* it. "Weary with the conflicts of the world, one goes into the Church to seek refreshment for the soul," wrote J. Gresham Machen, a Fundamentalist leader of the twenties; ". . . alas, too often, one finds only the turmoil of the world." Activists may be tempted to see in this attitude a kind of conservatism by default, and defenders of the *status quo* have at times been only too happy to see the church withdraw from involvement with and judgment upon the world. Among those, liberals as well as conservatives, who feel that modern man has become excessively politicized, Machen's appeal may strike a more responsive chord. Donald Meyer argued in *The Protestant Search for Political Realism* (1960), that the churchly liberals themselves came one day to realize that the real conflict within the soul of twentieth-century man was not between moral (liberal?) man and immoral (conservative?) society but between, in Meyer's terms, "concrete man" and "abstract society"; therefore, "the final upshot of the social gospel was that the gospel had to be more personal."

This was to move the argument up to a level at which only the most sophisticated of Fundamentalists—a J. Gresham Machen, trained at Marburg and Göttingen, not a Bryan—could have followed it. In any event the showdown between Fundamentalism and Modernism in the twenties was not directly over political doctrines either Left or Right, but over the theory of evolution. Whether Fundamentalism be at bottom liberal or conservative or neither of these in the political sense, was it not skewed in the direction of intolerance (a trait the liberal is prone to define as conservative, and vice versa) by its innate hostility to science?

There is obviously some justice in this view, as the tactics of the antievolution crusade made evident. Yet to accept it fully would be to overrate the persuasive power of the scientific tenets to which Fundamentalism was opposed. There was and is a widely held belief that the decrees of science are self-executing: pit the Bible and the *Origin of Species* against each other in fair and open combat and the truth, whatever it may be, will out. Hence anybody (other than one of Mencken's "gaping primates") who had once been exposed to the theory of evolution, unless deterred by considerations of convenience or opportunism—his neighbors might all be Fundamentalists, or he might be an Elmer Gantry—must accept the scientific truth and cease forthwith to be a Fundamentalist. The trouble with this kind of reasoning is that it expects too much of pedagogy, informal or formal.

In the twenties as later the scientific *method* was rarely taught systematically to the nonscientist. The textbook used by John Thomas Scopes in the high school at Dayton, Tennessee, is a case in point. One paragraph of Hunter's *Civic Biology* was subheaded "The Doctrine of Evolution"; a sentence within it began with the words "Geology teaches . . . ," and the sentence following commenced with "The great English scientist, Charles Darwin . . ." The student was, in short, being taught a dogma based on authority: "Science says" in place of "Thus saith the Lord." Even this catechism version of the theory was deleted from the next edition of Hunter. Judith Grabiner and Peter Miller have shown "Effects of the Scopes Trial," *Science*, 185 (Sept. 6, 1974) that after 1925 references to evolution disappeared from major high school biology texts. Students in the thirties and forties actually learned *less* about the controverted theory than they could have in Scopes's time! They could have gleaned more factual information about it from their science fiction magazines.

In 1957, after the launching of Sputnik I, efforts were made in America to bring secondary school science texts up to date. Sir Charles Snow in his *Two Cultures* essay (1959) ominously warned that the gap between the language of science and the language of the humanities and of "common sense" might have opened so far as to have become unbridgeable; many a literary intellectual, judging from his uncritical enthusiasm for F. R. Leavis's critique of Snow, seemed at times not to *want* to understand science, in as cranky and closed-minded a way as any Fundamentalist.

All that lay far in the future at the time of *Tennessee* v. *John Thomas Scopes*. Few Americans, intellectual or otherwise, realized the profundity of the revolution that was sweeping through science in the twenties. An exception was the Harvard physicist-philosopher Percy Bridgman, who confessed in a *Harper's* article in 1929 that "the physicist finds himself in a world from which the bottom has dropped clean out; as he penetrates deeper and deeper it eludes him by the unsportsmanlike device of just becoming meaningless." Yet the Modernists (as the Fundamentalists' opponents called themselves) proceeded as if the old monistic certitudes of nineteenth-century science still existed. Their task was complicated by the fact that the twenties were also a low point in the scientists' own efforts to understand and verify the process of evolution. Some of the more perceptive of the champions of orthodoxy knew this; with a debater's killer-instinct, Alfred W. McCann in the first chapter of his bombastic tract *God—or Gorilla?* attacked the credibility of "Piltdown Man," and to the chagrin of the Darwinists that particular fossil was in due course shown to be a fraud.

In a symposium of reminiscences of the Scopes trial forty years afterward, Lamont C. Cole, chairman of the Zoology department at Cornell, commented on his father's deposition as an expert witness at the trial: "As I compare that statement with the account of human evolution found in a leading college textbook of zoology published more than a quarter of a century later, I am impressed by the firm and definite conclusions that could be drawn in 1925 from the then scanty fossil evidence." Since scientific hypotheses come and go, Fundamentalists were therefore able to argue, why should anyone accept an evolutionary theory which might be supplanted tomorrow, in preference to "the Faith once delivered to the saints"?

Of course few of the Fundamentalists, and few of the Modernists, one must add in all fairness, could have appreciated a critique with the dialectical subtlety of Louis T. More's *The Dogma of Evolution*, nor would most of them have been aware of the confession of the British geneticist Sir William Bateson before the American Association for the Advancement of Science that discussions of evolution had come to an end "primarily because it was obvious that no progress was being made. . . . Variation of many kinds, often considerable, we daily witness, but no origin of species" (*Science* [January 20, 1922]). If rural folk in particular distrusted the theory of evolution, it may not have been because they found it unnatural —any farmer who has bred stock knows there is *something* in the idea!—or because they knew how incomplete the scientists' own knowledge was, especially with regard to fossil man, but rather because the articulate propaganda for the theory was emanating from city pulpits, city universities, and city textbook publishers.

Do we return, then, in the last analysis to the hypothesis of rural-urban conflict in order to interpret Fundamentalism? McLoughlin's and Sandeen's point about the urban genesis and leadership of that movement (for example, the faculty and alumni of the Moody Bible Institute in Chicago) remains well taken, but we must not forget that people who move to the city do not necessarily cease to be country people. On one occasion the flamboyant evangelist Aimee Semple McPherson, who represented a successful fusion of Fundamentalism's rejection of the world, the flesh, and the devil with a nascent Hollywood culture's triumphant affirmation of all three, walked onto the stage of her Four-Square Gospel temple in Los Angeles carrying a full milk pail and asked her hearers how many of them had ever lived on a farm; Carey McWilliams, in his essay for *The Aspirin Age* (1949), reported that the entire audience stood up.

George E. Mowry has asserted of the twenties: "It was during those years that the country first became urban, particularly in the cast of its mind, in its ideals, and in its folkways." The census statistics for 1920 convincingly support that judgment, but they are based upon a conceptual fallacy. In that census more than half the population of the United States for the first time in its history was counted as urban, but an urban community was defined as any having more than twenty-five hundred people. By that definition, Sinclair Lewis's "Gopher Prairie" was urban! Such a statistic is, in fact, ahistorical; there had been urban forces shaping America prior to the twenties, for example in the Philadelphia of Benjamin Franklin, and there were rural influences at work in America after the twenties, for example in the Nashville of Hank Williams.

For all the onrush of urbanism from the twenties down through the seventies, we must keep in mind the persistence of ruralism, often at a more highbrow level than that of Fundamentalism. Joseph Wood Krutch, the sometime Columbia professor and *Nation* drama critic, moved to Arizona to observe the behavior of birds and lizards, and many of his friends who remained in or near New York close to what one of them called "God's concrete" afterward enlisted in the nature oriented movement we loosely term ecology, formerly called conservation. Aldo Leopold's land ethic has only recently been discovered, by thousands of new readers of his *A Sand County Almanac* (1949) but Leopold was already writing in the twenties. An urban socialist thoroughly attuned to industrial society, Harvey Swados, confessed in 1961 "I am of the city but not for it, for the countryside but not of it" and on a day in early June 1965 that seeker after consensus Lyndon B. Johnson paused from deploying warships and jet planes, the spearheads of an urban-industrial technology, to recall the hills of his West Texas boyhood: "Sometimes, in the highest councils of the nation, in this house [the White House], I sit back and I can almost feel that rough, unyielding, sticky clay soil between my toes." "The city stalks the country," a country poet has written, and for psychic purposes almost any kind of American can be a rustic at one time or another.

MEGALOPOLIS VERSUS GOPHER PRAIRIE

In our first chapter we touched upon the ambivalence of the archetypal Henry Ford between the future and the past; this was also, of course, an ambivalence as between town and country. In the words of the Nevins and Hill study, "Ford the countryman, the son of farming people, the child of Springwell Township lately wrested from the forest," who in fact had gone off to Detroit as a youth because he greatly preferred tinkering with machinery to farming, "was projected to leadership of the industrial and urban age." All his life the man who had done so much to bring the city to the farm faced emotionally in both directions. Mechanization would not lead to a "cold, metallic sort of world in which great factories will drive away the trees, the flowers, the birds and the green fields," Ford declared in *My*

Life and Work (1923); on the contrary, "unless we know more about machines and their use . . . we cannot have the time to enjoy the trees and the birds and the flowers, and the green fields." For Henry Ford, Roderick Nash concludes, "the machine and the garden were not incompatible." In affirming that compatibility Ford again and again lost himself in contradictions.

Frank Lloyd Wright, too, although dedicated to full use of the materials and construction methods appropriate to the Machine Age, wrote in 1910 of the "ignoble parasitism" on European architectural models by Americans as being "more characteristic of the Eastern citizen on the cinder-strip than [of] the Western citizen of the great prairies." At the beginning of the twenties he was turning from the style of the prairie houses he had built in his beloved Midwest to forms even less urban in their inspiration, houses in California and Arizona which recalled Mayan temples in the jungles of Yucatán or the natural topography of the desert itself. It is only necessary to compare Wright's work in the twenties with Weimar Germany's *Bauhaus* and its uncompromisingly mechanistic and aseptic canons of design to be reminded that throughout a long and vigorous career the prairie architect reminisced of boyhood summers on Grandfather's farm, complete with buzzing bees and new-mown hay.

Frank Lloyd Wright wrote and spoke of his antiurban organicism as "democracy in overalls"; Hiram Wesley Evans, Imperial Wizard of the Ku Klux Klan, in a much anthologized statement of 1926, complained against encroachment of the new urban civilization on behalf of the " 'rubes' and 'hicks' and 'drivers of second-hand Fords'," linking these people emotionally with the democrats in overalls who had been associated with the political fortunes of Jackson and Lincoln and Bryan. Jeffersonian liberals who rejected the rest of the Klan's ideology could share in this emotional linkage; William E. Dodd, subsequently FDR's ambassador to Germany, warned in a 1927 baccalaureate address of the rise of "an American peasantry already jeered at all over the country as morons and yokels . . . dirty, ill clad men and women, millions of them producing the foodstuffs of the great country of Washington and Jefferson." This was no time for "complacent big-city politics," Dodd declared; "Southern men and western leaders might well take stock of their resources, and seek a new deal in the politics of the time."

Properly, even the Klansmen should be seen as ruralist, rather than necessarily as rural. In a study of the Ku Klux Klan in Texas during the twenties, Charles C. Alexander showed that "the Klan achieved its greatest strength and its most notable successes in the booming cities," among "Texans who found themselves living in a rapidly changing urban environment but clinging to the values of their rural background." Kenneth T. Jackson, studying *The Ku Klux Klan in the City, 1915–1930*, (1967) uncovered Klansmen in environments even more urban —at least forty thousand of them in Chicago alone. Our sympathy quickly cools when we learn that it was only the Nordic American for whom Imperial Wizard Evans spoke. The common men enrolled in the Ku Klux Klan, whether in a city klavern or on a country hillside, acknowledged no solidarity with such other categories of common men as, for example, immigrants, blacks, Jews, Catholics, or northeastern city dwellers. Taking this fact together with Henry Ford's private police, his hostility to labor unions, or his anti-Semitism, and also with Frank Lloyd Wright's apotheosis in fiction by Ayn Rand as a hero of the ultra-Right, it would be very easy to fall into the familiar stereotyped view that urban-rural conflict reduces to a struggle between humane civilization and something very like Fascism. Nevertheless, the present writer submits that to do so would be seriously to misread the history of the twenties, if not of modern America as a whole.

In saying this, he dissents from a strong trend within his guild. Morton and Lucia White, in their luminous essay *The*

Intellectual versus the City: From Thomas Jefferson to Frank Lloyd Wright, (1962) described an antiurban bias endemic among American thinkers, yet it is significant that of the dozen persons whom they discuss in some depth only one or perhaps two can be classified essentially as historians. The historiographic tendency in recent years has been to assume, not merely that the traditional American myth of agrarian virtue pitted against metropolitan vice is untrue, but that something very like the reverse is true: namely, that the city in America has had to fight to sustain its humane values against the onslaughts of a mean-spirited and narrow-minded ruralism. In many a monograph, whatever was narrow, corrupt, and vicious in rural life has been deemed typical, and whatever was tolerant, large minded, and rational in city life has also been considered typical. There is real danger that in revising the agrarian myth we shall end with the disconcerting discovery that our heroes and villains have simply changed places, to the detriment of historical insight.

A single crucial example will illustrate the point. We have already observed that the high school science textbook out of which John Thomas Scopes taught the theory of evolution was not remarkably scientific; what is even more ironical, considering that the American Civil Liberties Union was in Scopes's corner at the trial, is that some of the doctrines it contained were positively illiberal. Two pages after the paragraph on evolution appeared a paragraph on the races of man, and the author, describing the "five races or varieties of man, each very different from the others," capped the list with "the highest type of all, the Caucasians, represented by the civilized white inhabitants of Europe and America." Thus if a high school student had been emancipated from religious superstition by reading this textbook's account of evolution, he ran the risk of becoming bound in the far more lethal superstition of race. The fact that the Scopes trial took place in the rural South, which did not need or care to learn its racism out of a textbook, must be paired with the fact that a national supplier of schoolbooks, with headquarters in New York, Cincinnati, and Chicago, in publishing Hunter's *Civic Biology* was furthering the propagation *en masse* of a doctrine it would be not unfair to refer to as urban racism.

Urban or "highbrow" racism was if anything more insidious than rural or "lowbrow" racism since it was more developed and systematic. It had a long pedigree in intellectual America, far antedating the twenties. Jurgen Herbst quotes Professor John W. Burgess of Columbia, speaking before the Kaiser in Berlin in 1907, as having said "Uncle Sam does not want such rabble for citizens" as Slavs, Czechs, Hungarians, and South Italians. The British historian Edward A. Freeman would have agreed; he wrote in 1882 that America's social problems might be solved if only "every Irishman [were to] kill a Negro and be hanged for it." The First World War only interrupted and dampened, but by no means extinguished, an American rhetoric of "Nordic," "Aryan," sometimes "Anglo-Saxon" racial supremacy fully as assured and dogmatic as anything then heard in Germany. In one respect, indeed, the war heightened this kind of bigotry. John Higham in *Strangers in the Land* (rev. ed., 1963) has shown how wartime two-hundred-percentism gathered up the old hit or miss American anti-Semitic prejudice into a fullblown ideology, such that Jews became linked in the minds of many fearful Americans both with "Bolshevism" and—a hideous irony!—with pro-Germanism.

But some Gentiles also were given the racist treatment. Textbooks of the twenties and for long afterward were filled with descriptions of those classic degenerate families the Jukeses and the Kallikaks, accounts which by ignoring environmental and stressing "instinctual" factors seemed to give the thesis of biological inheritance of superior and inferior mental and even moral traits a scientific rationale. The newly developed and only half-understood intelligence tests used on Army recruits in the recent war seemed to give this racist thesis real statistical substance, and attracted to it men of the stature of Edward L.

Thorndike and Lewis Terman, psychologists; Henry Pratt Fairchild, professor of sociology at New York University; Paul Popenoe, editor of the *Journal of Heredity* and afterward a nationally known sex and marriage counselor; and many others. "It is natural," writes Thomas F. Gossett, "that in the histories of [the twenties] the views of the extremists have been accorded more attention, but it was mainly the academic writers on racial differences who made racism respectable." A good many of those academic writers held tenured chairs in urban universities.

This suggestion that the substitution of a half-understood Darwinism for a half-understood Bible could have led to an intellectualized racism is not fanciful. Henry Fairfield Osborn, director of the American Museum of Natural History where he aroused the wrath of Fundamentalists in 1926 with a vivid exhibit on the Age of Man, and author of a popular evolutionist tract *The Earth Speaks to Bryan*, agreed to testify at the Scopes trial as an expert witness for science; but in other quarters Osborn was better known for his campaigns for immigration restriction to keep the population balance in the United States predominantly Nordic. When Walter Lippmann, for example, took issue with men of high scientific standing and denied that mental ability was largely a matter of inheritance, the Harvard psychology professor William MacDougall declared that Lippmann was "denying also the theory of organic evolution, and he should come out openly on the side of Mr. Bryan."

"A man did not need to read an article or book on the biological, anthropological, psychological, or sociological aspects of race in order to participate in a race riot," Gossett concedes. "Still, ideas have a way of trickling down." If general historical and scientific information had its popularizers, as we noted in a previous chapter, so did "scientific" racism. There were Madison Grant's *The Passing of the Great Race* (1916), Harvard geneticist Edwin East's *Heredity and Human Affairs* (1927), and *The Rising Tide of Color* (1920) and other such works by Lothrop Stoddard, whose writings were on the whole favorably reviewed, by *The New York Times* and the *Bookman* among others. For that matter there were the fictional accounts like *The Red Napoleon* (previously discussed in a different context) and the British thriller that chronicled the career of *The Insidious Dr. Fu-Manchu*, whose untiring efforts to upset "the balance which a wise providence has adjusted between the white and yellow races" went into its fifth American printing in 1920 and whose exploits would still be selling briskly in paperback and on film forty years later, while Americans confronted a real China even more formidable, if rather less colorful, than the one created in the vivid imagination of Sax Rohmer.

In one sense at least, the racism of the twenties was far more vicious in its effect than that of the seventies. The latter, with one or two vehemently controverted exceptions, had few intellectual defenders, and when challenged usually had to retreat into blind irrationality or frankly acknowledged prejudice; so a tale like that of the evil Chinese doctor could be taken and read for what it was, a fantasy. Racism in the twenties, apart from the pioneering anthropological studies of race by Alês Hrdlicka and Franz Boas which would in due course undermine and discredit the concept, seemed to have the thoughtful, documented sanction of competent scholarship. As a result, racial bias was strengthened throughout the formal Establishment. Jewish quotas were established for admission to universities, particularly in the East, during this period, and Ellery Sedgwick, editor of the venerable *Atlantic Monthly*, was reluctant to publish the essays which were to become *The Modern Temper* on the ground that "the attitude is typical of the Jewish intellectual." Mr. Krutch, an Aryan native of Kentucky descended from a German refugee of 1848 named Krützsch, commented in his autobiography: "If blond Nordics (even though not Bostonian) were entertaining any such thoughts as mine there could be no telling what the world would come to."

Of course it was not only in Establishment circles that racist attitudes could be found in American cities during the twenties.

Discrimination by a college fraternity or a literary magazine or a summer resort might be an imposition and an inconvenience, but discrimination by a trade union, for example, could strike at survival itself. Irving Bernstein in *The Lean Years*, a history of the American worker during the twenties and early thirties, noted that technically the American Federation of Labor banned racial discrimination, but that in practice the power of admission to union membership rested with the internationals. "The Boilermakers and Machinists, for example, got around [the ban] simply by incorporating a racial clause in their rituals, binding members to propose only white workmen for membership." C. W. Chesnutt, testifying before a Senate subcommittee in 1928, was blunt: "I make the charge baldly that the labor unions of the United States, broadly speaking, are unfriendly to Negro labor, and I challenge them to prove the contrary."

Still more disquieting, in the light of developments since the twenties, was the emergence of overtly racist attitudes among urban blacks themselves. Marcus Garvey, a Jamaican who came to the United States with a "Back-to-Africa" plan for American Negroes, praised Warren Harding for a speech delivered in Birmingham in 1921 against racial amalgamation, and later supported a back-to-Africa bill sponsored by the unspeakably race-baiting Senator Theodore G. Bilbo of Mississippi; black pride, the mirror image of the white man's, demanded that the races separate. Garvey ruled his Universal Negro Improvement Association, writes John Hope Franklin, "with the assistance of one Potentate and one Supreme Deputy Potentate" and such orders as "the Knights of the Nile, the Knights of the Distinguished Service Order of Ethiopia, and the Dukes of the Niger and of Uganda"—not so very far from the world of Grand Dragons, Great Titans, King Kleagles, Kludds, Klaliffs, and Klokards presided over by Hiram Wesley Evans; the Klan, for the opposite of Garvey's reasons, openly supported the Garvey movement. "Garveyism was for the most part decisively repudiated by the Negro intellectuals" of the Harlem Renaissance, concedes E. David Cronon in his study of Marcus Garvey, *Black Moses*, but this "escapist program of chauvinistic Negro nationalism" (Cronon calls it) seems nevertheless to have had a wide popular following among Harlem Negroes: "To know Garvey is, in a sense, to understand the Negro world of the Twenties." Garvey scholarship in the years since Cronon's book was published has heartily concurred, except that Garvey's program now is less likely to be called "escapist." On the contrary, some black scholars would argue that those who *rejected* any back-to-Africa movement were the real escapists.

Racism then, like other forms of man's inhumanity to man in the twenties, was found on metropolitan campuses as well as in rural high schools, in labor unions as well as in business associations, in fashionable suburbs as well as in small towns (What right had Darien to complain about Gopher Prairie?), and above all in the city as well as in the country. Unlike some of the other social phenomena characteristic of the twenties this one has unfortunately not become dated or quaint. It survived into our own day, not only in the race riot and the slum ghetto and the segregated building trades union, but also, down to 1965, on the lawbooks, in the immigration legislation written into statute in the twenties.

Less drastic in operation than the laws for the sterilization of defectives enacted during the same period, constitutionally upheld by Mr. Justice Holmes on the ground that society should have the right to "prevent those who are manifestly unfit from continuing their kind" (*Buck* v. *Bell*, 274 U.S. 200, 1927), this legislation was equally eugenist in intent. Americans could plausibly have argued that a declining industrial labor force had no room for foreign workers even in a time of prosperity, and in a time of depression Franklin Roosevelt, or one of his ghost writers, was to declare: "We are not able to invite the immigration from Europe to share our endless plenty. We are now providing a drab living for our own people." But the "quota" system, whereby the *proportions* of the various nationalities or, in the more extreme view, "races" as they existed in the United States were to be maintained unchanged in what little immigration would still be permitted, clearly favored the "superior" ethnic stocks from the north and west of Europe, and reduced to a trickle the flow from the "inferior" south and east. The cultural effect was devastating. "Diversity made immigrant Chicago vivid 50 years ago," said the novelist Saul Bellow in a 1972 lecture at the Chicago Public Library (part of a centennial series on "The City in Historic and Philosophical Context"). Then, said Bellow, "the immigration laws of the '20's stopped the flow of laborers, shopkeepers, confectioners, upholsterers, cabinet makers, cooks, knife-sharpeners, umbrella repairmen, fruit peddlers, street-harpists, and waffle-wagon drivers who once filled the streets of Chicago. . . . As time has deprived the city of its culture, so has it stolen its individuality."

An exception perforce to the general national policy, owing to American colonialism, was immigration from the Philippine Islands, which multiplied ten times during the decade 1920–30. Maldwyn Allen Jones commented in closing a chapter on the demand for restriction in his study of immigration in American history that the whole melancholy history of the immigration controversy prior to the twenties was now repeated in miniature, with anti-Filipino demonstrations in California and Washington and a not entirely disinterested drive for Philippine independence.

The Congress of the United States, in deciding to write off the Philippine military campaign of 1899–1902 as a bad job and set the islands free, and in enacting so fundamental a reversal of America's historic policy toward the foreign-born as the national origins system represented, did not in any clear-cut way divide on liberal and conservative lines. If the Senate had heard racist arguments for the immigration restriction bill passed in 1897 couched in the Beacon Hill accents of the elder Henry Cabot Lodge, a conservative to his fingertips, it had also heard the almost equally conservative President Grover Cleveland strike down that bill with one of his typically plain spoken vetoes. Similar bills had been blocked by the determined actions of the more or less conservative Taft and the more or less liberal Wilson. Among the "progressives," a term whose definition is beginning to pose an even greater problem for historians of modern America than "liberal" and "conservative," immigration restriction had long been an important objective, and William Leuchtenburg has pointed out that when the moment of truth came in 1924, not a single "progressive" vote in Congress was cast against the bill. Was this the Ku Klux Klan mentality in action, defending the purity of an agrarian America against alien contamination? We have been told over and over again by modern historians of Progressivism that the animus of that reform movement, by contrast with Populism, was urban.

In summation, bigotry and intolerance in the twenties were not a rural monopoly; equally a case could be made that humanitarianism and enlightenment—compare the metropolitan Hearst newspapers with the bucolic Emporia (Kansas) *Gazette*—were not entirely urban. It was as one country boy to another that the *Gazette*'s editor, William Allen White, having just finished reading *Main Street* aloud with Mrs. White, wrote to Sinclair Lewis on November 23, 1920, "to tell you what a noble thing you have done" and declared that if he were a millionaire he "would go and bribe the legislature of Kansas to make 'Main Street' compulsory reading in the public schools." The Sage of Emporia seems also to have been on reasonably genial terms with that passionate antiruralist H. L. Mencken— data that do not fit the stereotype either of the city stalking the country or of the country strangling the city. Then, too, if Richard Hofstadter was right in saying that "life-adjustment educators would do anything in the name of science except encourage children to study it," it may well be that all the antievolution statutes threatened or enacted in all of rural or rural-minded America put together have not blighted as many budding young minds as have the dedicated disciples of the "new education" who in the twenties came charging out over the land from one metropolitan teachers' college.

The foregoing analysis has been intended as a correction of the historian's tendency to dwell upon the regressive features of American rural culture, and to neglect the equally unsavory aspects of the metropolitan past—a tendency that Mario S. DePillis, in a paper read before the Mississippi Valley Historical Association in 1965, deplored as "the chauvinism of the urban historians, who seem to believe that for urban history to rise, rural history must fall." In understanding the rural-urban polarity in America, for the twenties or for any other time, nothing is gained if we merely reverse the plus and minus signs. Town and country as unmitigated opposites—the world of *Main Street*, let us say, as against the world of *Manhattan Transfer*—can be understood historically only from a point of view which transcends them. In the rapidly urbanizing environment of the seventies, this may be more easily said than done, but the effort is nevertheless necessary.

On making the effort we may find that the polarity is not as absolute as it has sometimes appeared to be. In a thoughtful review of the Whites' *The Intellectual versus the City*, William H. Jordy suggested that the antiurban writers in America have embraced values that were not really small-town or rural at all: "If the city has been attacked, have intellectuals been substantially kinder to farming?" What they really wanted was a "metropolitan arcadianism, which differs from the folksiness of small-town attitudes in its emphasis on civilized values and a fundamentally complex social organization"—and very often the agrarian utopias have come down in reality to no more than "the suburban community, but without the chore of daily commuting."

Leo Marx has another name for the tragic response of American men of letters to the machine's invasion of the garden: "complex pastoralism." Without the complexity, the intellectual's pastoralism could become grotesque, as when the

Rhode Island fantasy writer and antiquarian Howard Phillips Lovecraft first saw the skyline of New York in 1922 and told his Manhattan host "that man is like the coral insect—designed to build vast, beautiful, mineral things for the moon to delight in after he is dead." The point of view is as inhumane as anything generated from within Megalopolis, for all its cosmic awe, and one is not surprised to find Lovecraft declaring elsewhere in the same paragraph, "I could not take humanity seriously if I wanted to." It is worth noting that the men who knew Lovecraft best have agreed that it took another and a far more traumatic, even tragic, stay in New York to mature him both as a writer and as a human being—"he came out pure gold," one of them declared afterward—even though he did in the end forsake the Babylonian towers on the Hudson for his own "pure New England lanes up which fragrant sea-winds sweep at evening."

As a matter of fact, the most informed misgivings about Megalopolis have always been articulated in Megalopolis itself. *Commonweal*, published in New York City, inaugurated its second year of publication on May 13, 1925, with a lead editorial on "The Terrible Super-City," prophesying an automated and dehumanized society along the lines made familiar to us by the culture criticism of more recent years. It is instructive for the present-day reader, fresh from our own discussions of the population crisis, to learn that a Catholic journal in the twenties could even then have raised the question "whether the limit of numbers permitting the community sense has not already been surpassed"; although the editorial asked if men could "stem the creation of monster communities with no soul, and work back to groups who know each other," it would be unthinkable to classify this liberal metropolitan weekly as antiurban.

The tragedy of any polar situation is that it becomes almost impossible for such balanced views to prevail. Instead it becomes a choice of Al Smith *or* Bryan, scientism *or* biblicism, immigrant *or* native, Wet *or* Dry, H. L. Mencken *or* Aimee Semple McPherson, Chicago gangster *or* Mississippi lyncher, bohemian *or* philistine. Town and country had found a common voice in America before, as when New York and Philadelphia workingmen rallied to Jackson or when Lincoln the backwoodsman campaigned successfully in the Cooper Union. They would find it again when a country squire from Hyde Park mastered the city machines and enlisted auto worker and farmer under the same banner. Still, for the decade of the twenties, town and country had lost the knack of speaking in concert, and shouted each other down.

To read what some man . . . has said about a great live book, this, which . . . we are all so jubilant over as a splendid way of saving labor, is probably as unstimulating and unfertilizing a process as the human mind can submit to. . . . It sets us all to writing books or judging of them with reference to other books that have already been written and judged, not with immediate reference to truths and thoughts. . . . No; read books themselves, and not men's talk about them. To read a book is to make a friend. To read a review is to be introduced to a passing stranger.

PHILLIPS BROOKS, late Bishop of Massachusetts (1875)

Suggestions for Further Study

This is not a formal bibliographic essay. The historian Burl Noggle, in the *Journal of American History*, 53 (September 1966): 299–314, documented a discussion of "The Twenties: A New Historiographical Frontier" so exhaustively, with footnotes which in turn lead one back to the notes of others, that to go over the same ground here would be in effect to compile a bibliography of a bibliography of bibliographies, an exercise in pedantic futility. The reader in search of an author or title referred to in the text but not discussed here may find what he is looking for by turning to the index; the writer has used this space instead for what a congressman would call "revising and extending my remarks for the *Record*."

The first comment is simply that in spite of all the historical monographs discussed in Noggle's essay and in this book there remains a great deal of work to be done on the twenties. Systematic economic history, except on the Crash itself, is one such area, a gap which is reflected in the text. The history of economic theory has been admirably covered by Joseph Dorfman in the fourth volume of *The Economic Mind in American Civilization* (New York, 1959), and there are thorough studies on individual businesses, such as automobiles, in Allan Nevins and Frank Ernest Hill, *Ford: Expansion and Challenge 1915–1933* (New York, 1957) and oil, in Harold F. Williamson *et al., The American Petroleum Industry*, II: *The Age of Energy, 1899–1959* (Evanston, Ill., 1959). Badly needed is the kind of monograph which would pull these two diverse sorts of inquiry together; indeed, to do justice to this subject would require a book far greater in bulk than the present one. Since the first appearance of this book the broader studies have begun to appear: David Brody has given us, for example, a fresh and sympathetic view of the "welfare capitalism" of the twenties (cited below). But the great work of synthesis is yet to come. I am surprised that the radical historians, who have given us such incisive comment on the Progressive economy and on that of the New Deal, have not focused more upon this important transitional era. One has but to read Charles and Mary Beard's summary in *America in Mid-Passage* (New York, 1939) of the post-Crash congressional investigations of the pre-Crash economy to realize that the evidence necessary for such a synthesis is there.

There are other gaps as well. It is typical, and noteworthy, that the authors of a symposium published in 1964 on *Change and Continuity in Twentieth Century America* when giving examples of the continuity tended to find them in the First World War (William E. Leuchtenburg), the Progressive Era (John Braeman), or even the nineties (Richard Leopold).

Allusions to the twenties in most of these articles were made in passing, as if the twenties had been an aberration, subordinate to an overall scheme of the twentieth century into which those years did not fit. Significantly, the editors of the Ohio State University Press's Modern America series, of which this symposium was the initial volume, scheduled as the second a collection of similar monographs specifically on the twenties; it was published in 1968, and although some of the articles in volume two were rehashes of their authors' own previous work, several of them—for example, David Brody's "A New Look at Welfare Capitalism," mentioned above, or David Burner's stimulating essay on the year 1919—are well worth reading.

If much work remains to be done on the twenties, still the past two decades have seen a quickening of interest in the period. The catalyst for much of this discussion, as more than one monographist has acknowledged, was Henry F. May, "Shifting Perspectives on the 1920's," *Mississippi Valley Historical Review*, 43 (1956): 405ff. The student would do well to begin by reading that luminous and literate essay. The present writer has in addition received a powerful conceptual stimulus from Leo Lowenthal's study, "Biographies in Popular Magazines," which is discussed at some length in the text; that article was reprinted without substantial change as "The Triumph of Mass Idols," chapter four in *Literature, Popular Culture, and Society* (Englewood Cliffs, N.J., 1961). Neither May nor Lowenthal was of course responsible for the particular responses of this writer to their creative influence.

Any hypothesis is subject to critical test. The reader is therefore invited to check the validity of the Lowenthal hypothesis (as used herein) against such contemporary studies of the twenties as the President's Research Committee on Social Trends, eds., *Recent Social Trends in the United States* (New York, 1933) and, on a smaller cross-sectional scale, Robert S. Lynd and Helen Merrell Lynd, *Middletown: A Study in American Culture* (New York, 1929). Similarly, the rural-urban polarity of which so much is made in our third chapter must be tested against that social trend of the twenties which was neither the one pole nor the other; a pioneering and still readable study is H. Paul Douglass, *The Suburban Trend* (New York, 1925). A more recent and polemical discussion is Lewis Mumford, "Suburbia and Beyond," chapter 16 in *The City in History: Its Origins, Its Transformations, and Its Prospects* (New York, 1961). Constance McLaughlin Green, *American Cities in the Growth of the Nation* (London, 1957), is important for background on particular cities—her account of Detroit is particularly insightful—and the work is free from the urban chauvinism of which Mario DePillis complained (see above, p. 103). "The middle years of the twentieth century . . . may constitute the last period of American history in which city influence will overshadow every other in the nation," Mrs. Green quite surprisingly concluded.

An even better way than reading the arguments of scholars to probe the concrete historical reality from which all sociological (and historical!) generalizations arise is to immerse oneself in the magazines of the twenties, both the mass media kind studied by Lowenthal and the news comment and culture criticism sort. Robert B. Luce has judiciously edited a selection from one journal in the latter category, *The New Republic*, entitled *Faces of Five Decades* (New York, 1964); pp. 54–175 deal with the twenties. In 1967 the newsmagazine *Time* launched a series of "*Time* Capsules," digesting selected years from its back files. Other such anthologies might be a worthwhile publishing venture, particularly if they excerpted not only those periodicals that have survived into our own time (*New Yorker, Commonweal*) but also, and even more instructively, those that have not (*The Literary Digest, World's Work*). The compendium by Cleveland Amory, *et al.*, from *Vanity Fair* (New York, 1960) was a step in that direction.

Still, useful as such collections are, nothing substitutes for a plunge into the files themselves. The reader is particularly fortunate who has access to bound volumes he can handle physically, without the subtle separation from reality inherent in the use of microfilm. He would do well to vary his diet of dated politics and literary opinion with some sampling of the specialized presses—religious (*Christian Century*, *Catholic World*), popular science (*Scientific American*), light satire (the old *Life*), and the like—not neglecting the so-called little magazines. He should also pay some attention to changing styles in advertisements, layout, typography, and artwork. What an imaginative examination of this kind of pictorial material can yield is demonstrated in the evolution of the flapper, as seen in magazine cover illustrations of the twenties—in a book with an otherwise rather conventional interpretation, following Allen: Elizabeth Stevenson, *Babbitts and Bohemians: The American 1920s* (New York, 1967). For the mass media publications, a useful account of their transformation from the times of the muckrakers to our own day is Theodore Bernard Peterson, *Magazines in the Twentieth Century*, 2d ed. (Urbana, Ill., 1964); selected individual magazines which spanned the years of the twenties may be studied in Frank Luther Mott's standard *A History of American Magazines*, vols. 4 and 5 (Cambridge, Mass., 1957).

These résumés should be used for historical perspective; they are in no way a substitute for the actual magazines. For more formal endeavors in the arts, both fine and lively, there is likewise no substitute for the work itself. The student is urged to read the novel, hear the jazz, see the play, walk through the building. Secondary discussion, particularly technical elucidation, as in Arthur Drexler's brief editorial introduction to *The Drawings of Frank Lloyd Wright* (New York, 1962) or as in explanations of the technique of motion-picture film editing, can be helpful, but it is intrinsically dangerous; even a photograph of a building can editorialize. For the twenties, it is hard to find a critical tract in any of these fields that is not, in some sense, partisan.

For a particularly extreme example, see almost everything that has been written about Ezra Pound. He and his work were declared *in* by the poetic *beau idéal* of the twenties, T. S. Eliot, who dedicated *The Waste Land* to Pound in 1922; *out* by the United States Army, which after Pound's pro-Axis broadcasts from Rome in the Second World War confined him in a detention stockade; *in* by a prize committee of the Library of Congress, and *out* by the *Saturday Review of Literature*, for the *Pisan Cantos* which Pound composed during that detention; and subsequently *in* and *out* and *in* once more in a running battle that was still raging at the time of the poet's death in 1972: see Michael Wood, "Ezra Pound," *New York Review of Books* (February 8, 1973): 7–11. This intellectual cat fight, including at least one public challenge to personal combat, has so totally befogged the issue under inky clouds of political righteousness, critical dogmas, and wounded *amour-propre* as to have moved the poet Karl Shapiro to declare in 1949 that "few poets anywhere [let alone the perplexed layman!] are in a position to say what they really think of Pound's work." Debates over literary or other personalities of the twenties do not ordinarily bring into collision so wide a range of antipathies and loyalties —patriotic, cultural, political, ethnic, institutional, cultic, and personal—as the Pound controversy so notoriously has. In lesser degree each reader must build his own defenses against the transient *ins* and *outs* of culture criticism (including the present writer's) in assessing almost any career or creation of the twenties.

One defense is to bear in mind the bewildering variety of what in fact was seen, done, heard, and read during the twenties; its best seller lists included both *Main Street* and Emily Post's *Etiquette*, both *The Story of Philosophy* and *Gentlemen Prefer Blondes*, both *Elmer Gantry* and *The Man Nobody Knows*, both *Magnificent Obsession* and *Believe It or Not*. They were banner years both for Ernest Hemingway and for Edgar Rice Burroughs, the creator of Tarzan. Another such check against the transitory critical absolutes is to study work which *was* the subject of high intellectual regard in the twenties but has since been dropped from the canon: James Branch Cabell is a prime example. Booth Tarkington's reputation has suffered a similar eclipse even though the world of his novel *Alice Adams* "was, for incomparably more people than Spain or Paris or the Ritz could possibly be, the 1920's"; see Winfield Townley Scott, "Tarkington and the 1920's," *American Scholar*, 26 (1957): 181–194. There is of course the danger that such uncanonical writers may one day be restored to favor, but in a misleading form; Cabell, in his 1965 avatar as paperback science fiction, may be an example. One final check, as two novels cited by the writer in the text confirm, is to pay some attention to the kind of art produced in the twenties which by almost any standard in almost any period could have been deemed bad.

After such a plunge directly into the crosscurrents of the twenties, not before, is the time to turn to the many solid and valuable secondary accounts such as: Carl W. Condit, *American Building Art*, II: *The Twentieth Century* (New York, 1961); Blanche H. Gelfant, *The American City Novel* (Norman, Okla., 1954), a study the writer found particularly helpful on Dos Passos; Chadwick Hansen, "Social Influences on Jazz Style: Chicago 1920–30," *American Quarterly* 12 (1960): 493ff.; Leland D. Peterson, "Ezra Pound: The Use and Abuse of History," *American Quarterly* 17 (1965): 33ff.; or Philip M. Wagner, "Mencken Remembered," *American Scholar*, 32 (1963): 256ff., to list only a few from a variety of fields. The reader should diligently search, in particular, for studies that present a view differing from that expressed in this book. An example is Philip Young, *Ernest Hemingway: a Reconsideration* (University Park, Pa., 1966), which treats that author's talent not primarily as a response to a world-historical situation but rather as an adaptation to an illness—an interpretation the present writer has consciously and deliberately eschewed. Caution: lest any student receive the impression that books and ideas were all there were to the twenties, let him read and reread Irving Bernstein's able and eloquent *The Lean Years: A History of the American Worker, 1920–1933* (Boston, 1960), and Gilbert Osofsky's trenchant study *Harlem: The Making of a Ghetto* (New York, 1966).

In warning against taking the cultural life of the twenties at second hand the present writer does not mean to imply that such accounts as, for example, Mark Schorer's monumental *Sinclair Lewis: An American Life* (New York, 1961) can be dispensed with: quite the contrary. Nevertheless, even so careful and balanced a work as Schorer's has its own special pitfalls. As Andrew Sinclair wrote in the *Manchester Guardian Weekly* for November 15, 1962, reviewing a similarly careful and balanced and exhaustive study by Arthur and Barbara Gelb of Eugene O'Neill: "The effect of this gigantic biography is curious. . . . the sum of the facts do not add up to the whole O'Neill. In 'Long Day's Journey Into Night,' he reveals himself more nakedly than his biographers." Some biographers recognize this problem, and allow their subjects to speak at length for themselves; a particularly effective example is Nancy Milford, *Zelda* (New York, 1970).

Indeed, for many of the leading figures of the twenties, and this goes for politicians as well as for literati, the writer is tempted to violate one of the most axiomatic assumptions of his guild. It goes without saying, as they say, that autobiography is inevitably self-serving, and never more artfully deceptive than when most "frank" and confessional; that the unpublished diary is more reliable than the most conscientious memoir, and the contemporary letter worth more credence still. Some diaries and letters do meet this test; the touching combination of fresh youthfulness with cloistered dedication in Ambassador Dwight Morrow's daughter comes through convincingly in *Bring Me A Unicorn: Diaries and Letters of Anne Morrow Lindbergh 1922–1928* (New York, 1971). To shake one's faith in the relative credibility of diaries it is only necessary to think of Count

Ciano; as for the utility of autobiography, who has more faithfully and accurately recorded the intentions of Herbert Hoover, for example, than Hoover's own *Memoirs*? The reader will have noticed that the writer has drawn heavily on autobiographies to invoke the spirit of the American twenties; when they are as culturally lively as Matthew Josephson's engagingly titled *Life Among the SurRealists* (New York, 1962); as sexually frank as Max Eastman's *Love and Revolution: My Journey Through an Epoch* (New York, 1964); as civilized as Margaret Mead's *Blackberry Summer* (Boston, 1973); as judicious and common-sensical as *More Lives than One*, by Joseph Wood Krutch (New York, 1962); or as joyous as *The Best Times*, by John Dos Passos (New York, 1966), their use for the interpretation of history requires no apology. They are cited especially in the first chapter of this work, out of a conviction that these reminiscent and articulate survivors by and large were more insightful in their understanding of the period than have been most of the younger people who have written books about them.

Where the problem of interpretation becomes murky is the point at which conjuring up a mood passes over into judgment on controverted points of fact. Mr. Justice Frankfurter by consulting a clear and well-organized memory, and John Dos Passos by dusting off his own crumbling pamphlets and adding interpretive comment for the new age, could re-create a sense of what it had felt like to work for the Sacco-Vanzetti Defense Committee; they could not finally settle the question of which bullet could/might/must have been fired from whose revolver. Ballistics tests of "Sacco's" weapon in 1961—the quotation marks are a measure of the stubbornness of the controversy—only touched off a new round of argument; see Francis Russell, *Tragedy in Dedham: The Story of the Sacco-Vanzetti Case* (New York, 1962), and, in rebuttal, Michael A. Musmanno, "The Sacco-Vanzetti Case: A Critical Analysis of the book 'Tragedy in Dedham' . . .", 11 *Kansas Law Review* 481 (1963). To take a less grim and racking example, it may well be true as Edgar

Kauffmann and Ben Raeburn asserted, in *Frank Llyod Wright: Writings and Buildings* (New York, 1960), that "Wright was able to recall the past with exceptional, detailed vitality" in his 1957 *Testament*—but do the roofs of those buildings leak or don't they?

It is in forming this kind of judgment that the historian comes at last to play his indispensable role. He may not finally settle the controversy; indeed, he probably will not, but he can assist the reader to chart the controversy's shape and define its terms. For example, beginning with Samuel Lubell's discussion in *The Future of American Politics* (New York, 1952), one of the most central controversies about the twenties, the presidential campaign of 1928, has received just such clarifying treatment. Some of this analytical literature is cited in the notes to the present writer's "The Campaign of 1928 Re-Examined: A Study in Political Folklore," *Wisconsin Magazine of History*, 46 (1963): 263ff. An aspect of the controversy not dwelt upon in that essay or in those cited sources was discussed by James H. Smylie in "The Roman Catholic Church, the State, and Al Smith," *Church History*, 29 (1960): 321ff.; and an important more recent monograph is David Burner's, "The Brown Derby Campaign," *New York History*, 46 (1965): 356ff. The papers of Al Smith were accidentally destroyed by a fire in Albany, and therefore—so one specialist in twentieth-century political history, Jordan A. Schwarz, has told the present writer—no definitive biography of Smith can ever be written; readers of this essay are invited to take that judgment as a challenge.

No historian can have the last word on any debatable aspect of the twenties by confining his attention to that brief decade alone. The John Kennedy episode has caused us to rethink the Al Smith episode; the affluence under Coolidge can instructively be compared with the affluence under Eisenhower; the stance of Secretary Kellogg is thrown into relief by the stance of Secretary Rusk; the scandal of Watergate was immediately likened by mass media commentators to the scandal of Teapot Dome. Indeed, for all the ritual absolution of themselves from the sin of present-mindedness, all the discussants of the twenties have brought the perspective of more recent events to bear. It was the great merit of Henry May's essay to have pointed this out. Most politically liberal historians, for example, consciously or unconsciously have judged the twenties from their prior knowledge that the Crash was just around the corner, and when a conservative occasionally has contested this view, as in John Chamberlain, *The Enterprising Americans: A Business History of the United States* (New York, 1963), he like the liberals has ended by assessing the pre-Crash economy from the standpoint of a judgment on the coming events of the New Deal.

In "The 1930's: America's Major Nostalgia" *The Key Reporter*, 38 (Autumn, 1972): 2–4, 8, Robert Nisbet contended that those New Deal years had, for the time being, supplanted the Jazz Age as the period most compelling to America's historical imagination. But nostalgias change. The forties have also lately had their innings (witness the success of films like *Patton* and *Summer of '42*); so have the fifties (witness the tributes logged on innumerable rock radio stations). In this kind of recycling the twenties' number is bound to come up again. Meanwhile, if the New Deal has modified men's interpretation of the twenties, so has the Second World War, as well as the Cold War, the New Frontier, the Great Society, the seething sixties. The seventies and eighties can be expected to contribute their own distinctive insights to an interpretation of the twenties. The next move, gentle reader, is up to you.

INDEX